CISSIE

Cissie

Football's most famous mother
Cissie Charlton
tells her story

with Vince Gledhill

Bridge Studios
Northumberland
1988

First published in Great Britain in 1988

by Bridge Studios
  Kirklands
  Scremerston
  Berwick upon Tweed
  Northumberland
  TD15 2RB

  Tel: 0289 302658/330274

This paperback edition first published in 1989 by Bridge Studios

ISBN 0 951263 0 9 9

Typeset and printed by Martin's of Berwick.

To my husband Bob

ACKNOWLEDGEMENTS

Sincere thanks to the following for photographs used in this book: Mr Bill Harrison, Mr Jack Wallace, G. B. Wade, the Newcastle Evening Chronicle & Journal Ltd, the *Daily Express*, the *Sun*, the *Manchester Evening News*, D. C. Thompson & Co Ltd, and the Football Association. Thanks also to Mr Vin Kearney for permission to use his poem 'Jack Rodway's Trolley'. Special thanks to Jack Charlton and his wife Pat.

FOREWORD

These fascinating memoirs of Cissie Charlton should be read by every mother who loves her children and is ambitious for them. The more you read this book you will realise the tremendous influence that a mother can exert on her sons and how they are not only successful in what they do, but what they are.

Cissie Charlton was the daughter of a miner and her father and grandfather were enthusiastic football players. When she was young, she could kick a ball as well as her brothers. She married a handsome miner, whose interest was boxing and he won a boxing match so that he could buy her a wedding ring.

Her first son was christened Jack and her second Robert, but he was always known as Bobby. Almost as soon as they could walk she took them to football matches and when Bobby was nine his grandfather said he would be a distinguished player.

At 15 Bobby was playing for Manchester United and he rose in the following years to become one of the great sportsmen of England. He was a sportsman in the best sense of the word as he was not concerned, as so many players are today, with money and publicity, but with the game itself.

He also had that magnetic aura of a star and though he never pushed himself, the moment he appeared on the ground, one's eyes instinctively went towards him. He was in fact, the great 'gentleman' player as a footballer, as never in all the years he was playing, were there uncomfortable incidents with the players or the referee which so often spoil matches today. Bobby Charlton's generosity to charity, besides the fact that he was capped 106 times for England is part of football history and he received first the OBE and then the CBE.

Mrs Charlton's story in itself is an example to all women. She fought courageously against cancer and what I think is so touching is that now a widow of over seventy finding life rather lonely and time hanging heavily on her hands, she was asked to help voluntarily in the local school.

When she did so a child said to her:

'Are you Bobby and Jack's mother?'

She said: 'Yes, I am,' proudly.

'Will you teach us,' the small boy said, 'to play football?'

This remarkable woman is doing exactly that.

Let us hope she will inspire many children to be as brilliant at the game and as fine sportsmen as her sons have been.

Barbara Cartland.

PROLOGUE

The boys on my team were seven and eight years old and I was more than seventy. But I didn't feel my age, so why should I act it, I asked myself?

Shouting all the way, we ran hell-for-leather up the school football pitch. They played and I refereed. 'Pass; use yer head; control it; dribble', I shouted. I had to make a lot of noise, because as well as referee, I was also coach and a spectator crowd of one.

It began to drizzle; a cold springtime drizzle, which in the North East, where I come from, has a special way of chilling to the bone. But we didn't care, the lads and me. We just kept running and playing the game until one of the women teachers came out of the school to order us back in. 'If those children don't catch their death of cold in this drizzle, then you certainly will,' she scolded.

My doctor had also warned me about my heart and given me some tablets, but they slowed me down so much that I became listless and thoroughly depressed. For the first time in my life, I actually began to feel like the old woman I see in the mirror every day and I didn't like it. I might be a white-haired, widowed granny who won't see seventy again (or seventy-five for that matter), but what's wrong with wanting to act young, even if you're not?

I ditched the tablets and went back to the football pitch and the little team I had been coaching at Coulson Park First School in my home town of Ashington, in Northumberland. Football was my first love and the way things are going it will be my last – and that suits me just fine.

My great-grandfather, my grandfather, my father (I always called him 'Faatha'), my four brothers, were all footballers. So was my cousin, Newcastle United's most famous centre-forward, 'Wor' Jackie Milburn. Two of my four sons, Bobby and Jack Charlton, also earned very special places in football history.

11

But in spite of my family background and my love of this great game, I was born a woman and that little twist of fate decided that here was one member of the Milburn clan who would not have a career in football. Daughter, wife and mother would be my role in life. Yet football was in my blood and it would not be denied.

The language, the history, the tactics and the personalities of the game were part of my upbringing and as familiar to me as to any man. So there was no way that I would ever be content as the 'little woman at home' who placidly listens while her menfolk talk about what happened on the pitch or the terraces. I wanted more than that. I needed to be there, I needed to be part of it. Whether it was on the terraces of Wembley, or the sidelines of a miners' welfare ground watching two local teams play – or even chasing up and down a school pitch with a team of tots. That, for the past seventy six years, is where I have wanted to be.

That has been *my goal*!

MY FAMILY TREE

Jack Milburn
(My Great-Grandfather)

Jack (Warhorse) Milburn

(Sons)   (Daughters)

Bob, 'Buck', Alec, Jack (Tanner), Jimmy, Sam   Cissie, Maggie, Florrie, Molly, Phyllis, (Unknown), (Unknown)

Family includes   (Sons)   (Daughters)

"Wor" Jackie Milburn   Jack, George, Jimmy, Stan   Cissie, Etty, Gladys

Jack, Bob, Gordon, Tom, (Charlton)

CHAPTER ONE

I was black – coal black. 'Hacky, mucky, dorty' was the popular Ashington expression for my state and, I can't deny, it fitted me to a tee.

To be fair, it was hard for a bairn like me to be in any other state as I romped on my favourite playpark – the local dumping ground for colliery shale and cinders from the coal mines in Ashington. In my first six years as far as I can recall, I was never away from that grimy adventure park outside our home at 180 Hawthorn Road. The shallow humps and hollows of waste and shale gave me and my two brothers George and Jack, all the scope we needed for every type of game our active imaginations could dream up, especially if it involved running, jumping, climbing or hiding.

Mother was less impressed. She did her level best to see that I was as neatly turned out as a good little girl was expected to be in those days. My aprons – we called them pinnies – were scrubbed spotless and always starched. Unhappily for me I too was scrubbed until I was pink-cheeked and just as dirt-free.

But she was fighting a losing battle. I just wasn't cut out to be one of those cute little china doll lasses. That was far too namby-pamby for me. I was a rough-and-tumble tomboy with no time for girls' toys or girls' games. Lads' games played on lads' terms and lads' territory – that was what I wanted. And why shouldn't I? I could kick a pig's-bladder football just as far and just as straight as any boy. I could run as fast and I could punch as hard as well. Still, it must have been tough on Mother, because there were times when my brothers and me went home in some filthy states, especially when it had been raining. But we were blissfully unaware of the toil and frustration we must have caused her.

I can't remember anything of my father in those days. I was still a toddler when he took the King's shilling and went off to fight a foreign foe who we called 'The Jarmans', in the First

15

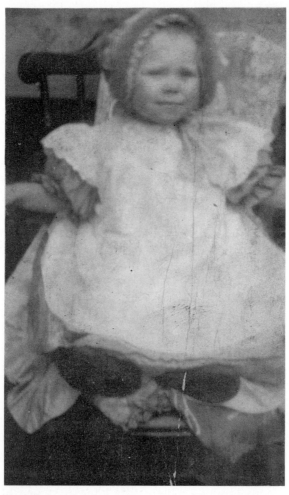

Me dolled up as every mother wants her baby daughter to look – but it didn't last.

World War. Soon afterwards he was a prisoner of the'Jarmans' after being captured on the Somme.

Mother was left to feed and clothe us until the end of the war on a pitifully small allowance, which she supplemented with pin money she earned by working at nights in a local fish and chip shop. It is a tribute to how well she managed that I don't remember those times as being especially hard. My biggest problem was in trying to find a game to play with my brothers which did not put the neighbours' windows at peril. With kids as boisterous as we were, that was no easy job!

Our Hawthorn Road home was modest even by the standards of those days. It was a downstairs flat in a half-mile long, soot-stained terrace. When I stood in my back lane the two walls of yellow Ashington bricks which flanked me, stretched so far into the distance in die-straight lines that they seemed to eventually meet and merge at the far end of the street. I lived with my parents and brothers in two downstairs rooms at Hawthorn Road. One was a combined kitchen/living room and the other was our only bed-room. Neither was very big and both had little in the way of furniture.

The family grew further, when I was four years old, with the birth of my sister Esther. She arrived shortly after Father went to war and was four before he had his first sight of her.

The flat above ours was rented by my Aunt Cissie who became a second mother to me. When my own mother worked at night in the fish shop it was Aunt Cissie who looked after us. During the daytime, when Aunt Cissie was at work, my own family swelled by another two as Mother in turn looked after Cissie's son and daughter, Mary and Jimmy.

Although she had been christened Elizabeth my aunt was only ever called Cis or Cissie. I was named Elizabeth after her, and for me too Elizabeth became and remained Cissie. We did differ in one respect, however. Aunt Cissie had picked up a liking for the clay pipe, probably from lighting up the one smoked by her mother, my old Granny Bess Milburn. But I have never enjoyed the smoking habit. My Aunt Cissie was not as blatant about her smoking, however, as Granny Bess who didn't care a fig who saw her with that nicotine-stained old pipe clamped between her gums.

Aunt Cissie's secretiveness about her own guilty enjoyment of smoking a clay pipe led to some comical moments when she was caught out. If anyone called at her flat unexpectedly when she was smoking she had a habit of shoving the lit pipe under the bib of her pinny. We kids knew fine well where it was and fully expected that at any moment her bust would burst into flames. At other times she tucked the pipe behind a framed photograph of her husband Charlie's favourite pigeon. It was odd enough to see that picture of his bird hanging where most people would have a treasured family portrait. But to see the smoke slowly curling upwards from behind it always had us torn between fits of giggles and the fear that at any time the picture was about to go ablaze and reduce Uncle Charlie's precious portrait to ashes.

Our flat and Aunt Cissie's shared a high-walled backyard and a wash-house in it. Inside the wash-house was a copper set-pot water boiler, built over a small coal fire, and a poss-tub.

Wash-day was always a major event in those days and there were chores aplenty, even for little tots of my age. My job was to grate a huge bar of blue speckled soap into flakes which would dissolve quickly when mixed with the laundry. (There was no such thing as soap powder.) Those were the days when nothing was wasted and an extra use could be found around the home for most items. Starch was one of them. It could be bought from stores in two forms – as a solid lump or as powder in a box. Mothers who bought the powder found that it doubled very nicely as baby talc.

Unfortunately I hadn't realised the difference when mother sent me to buy some at the corner shop and I got a flea in my ear for bringing home a solid lump of the stuff. But I refused to take the blame entirely. To my stubborn way of thinking, the shop-keeper should somehow have known exactly what Mother had wanted and not sold me the wrong starch in the first place.

Even as a bairn I was blunt-speaking (and I haven't changed much) so I stormed out of the house and went back to the shop with the offending lump of starch. I stamped into the store and

Tuesday was wash day and as well as grating soap I had to have a go at the poss-tub (like Florrie Anderson here). But for me it meant standing on a stool to reach. I had to poss 100 times, have a rest, and then another 100 times!

yelled: 'You shouldn't have given me this. I wanted the stuff for the bairn's arse!'

Another prized item with a double use in those lean days was the wooden barrel. These were used to deliver fat to fish shops, but once empty they made ideal poss-tubs. One cooper even made himself a healthy living just touring the pit rows renovating barrels when they began to wear out.

Monday was always wash-day and it really did take the whole day. The worst wash-day job for mother and the rest of the miners' wives was cleaning their men's work clothes. These had first to be 'dadded' against a wall to shake off the loose dirt in choking clouds of coal dust and dried mud. Then they had to be soaked overnight in soda and water before being dumped, along with the grated soapflakes, into the poss-tub. The tub stood about three feet high and three feet wide and was half-filled with hot

19

water carried from the set-pot. 'Possing' was done with a 'poss-stick', a 10lb stump of wood with stout prongs at its base and a handle at the top which could be grasped firmly with two hands. Its design meant that the poss-stick could be raised and lowered and twisted from side to side in a single flowing motion. Finally the clothes were scrubbed with a stiff brush. Whites were boiled and blued in fresh cold water before being squeezed through the twin rollers of a mangle.

All this was back-breaking work, but just one of the tasks which men and women alike accepted as part of the housewife's lot then.

Bath-night in the Milburn household always began with heating water, usually by the kettleful, over our big open coal fire. Then, a long, galvanised metal bath was unhitched from a nail on the yard wall and set in front of the kitchen fire to be filled with hot water. It was an exhausting ritual which, even now, makes me appreciate the true luxury of having hot water available on demand. Even to this day I think that one of life's great pleasures is to be able to fill a hot bath at the turn of a tap.

It didn't occur to me at the time, but I am amazed to remember now just how clean our Hawthorn Road home was in those days. Even our wooden kitchen table was scrubbed lily-white. Mother was very houseproud, but she faced a monumental task. Streets at that time were not made up and consisted of just dirt tracks which on rainy days became filthy quagmires. Our word for it was 'clarty'. Muck was always being carried in on our shoes and clothes. There was no avoiding it, but it must have been heart-breaking for women like Mother. There was little enough for a pitman's wife to take pride in, but the neatness with which she kept her home was a point of honour. As a result many were fanatically houseproud and the mess from the unmade streets outside only added to their troubles.

Not for many years did the miners of Ashington, including my father, know the relief of being able to leave their body grime at work, courtesy of the pithead baths. Instead, it all came home and had to be scrubbed off there – at least, most of it came off.

Some miners were very fussy about having their backs washed.

Mother's nightmare. The back streets of Ashington, which became a clarty mess when it rained.

Many were firmly convinced that too much washing weakened them and usually had a black square of untouched coal dust on their backs. No doubt my own father would have been the same, although I remember nothing of him from those days.

I was just two years old when Archduke Franz Ferdinand, the heir to the throne of Austria-Hungary, was shot and the First World War broke out in 1914. Few families across Europe escaped its effects and mine was no exception.

Before I was old enough to be aware of him going, Father had joined the Tyneside and Scottish regiment and vanished from our lives for the next four years. Yet with a child's ability to adapt and cope, I simply accepted his absence and put it out of my mind.

Soon after going to the front, Father was taken prisoner on the Somme. The fact that he survived long enough during a battle in which thousands of British soldiers were slaughtered was due to an ironic twist of fate. A British artillery shell landed by his side as he ran towards the enemy lines. By some miracle, shrapnel from it missed Father, but he was stunned and trapped under a

21

mass of earth which rained down on him in the explosion. Eventually he was dug out by a squad of German soldiers who argued among themselves whether to bother to take him prisoner or just stick a bayonet in him there and then. He was lucky; they decided to let him live. Back home in Ashington we were largely untouched by the war, except for 14 April 1915, when I was two and a half years old.

As usual I was playing on the spoil ground outside my house and I remember looking up and seeing a grey shape floating in the sky. It was a German Zeppelin. It was the first I had seen and as I stared it flew south of my play park and headed further inland. It had come in over the North Sea and was following the course of the river Wansbeck.

Moments later my panic-stricken mother ran to my brothers and me and shepherded us away. Other women had run onto the field for their children and some of the mothers pulled their pinnies over their heads in blind terror.

They were never in any danger, the Zeppelin was too far away for that, but other people were not so lucky. A few minutes later, a bomb was dropped on the neighbouring village of West Sleekburn. Moments after that three more were released on the next village of Choppington. Ten more rained down on Bedlington before the Zeppelin turned south and headed for Blyth, then Cramlington. At Seaton Burn two more were dropped. At Wallsend a child was hurt by one of eight bombs dropped towards Tyneside shipyards.

On 11 November 1918, my sixth birthday, the First World War ended. It puzzled me for many years afterwards when people cried on my birthday. I just wanted to celebrate and they were so sad.

In that same year of 1918 we moved to a colliery house at 281 Sycamore Street. Moving house – we always called it 'shiftin' – was done in those days by flat cart, sometimes pulled by the local rag-and-bone man's horse and sometimes by hand. One blessing for women like my mother, whose man was away at the war, was that in those friendly pit rows, help never had to be sought. It was offered automatically.

The old saying often used about people falling on hard times was that they had been left to 'God and good neighbours'. Ashington was a town of 'good neighbours', so when shifting day came along there was no shortage of friends and relations to see that we and our bits of furniture and clothes were safely delivered to our new home.

Flat carts heaped with possessions became a regular sight over the years as more and more colliery houses were built for the town's still-growing workforce. One cart, owned by an Ashington shopkeeper called Jack Rodway, was hauled through the town so much over the years – and with such a selection of cargoes, including, at least once, a boat – that it became a celebrity in its own right. Jack Rodway's trolley even had a monologue written about it by dialect poet Vin Kearney.

It goes:-

Noo a'll tell ye aboot a trolley that was once of local fame.
It belonged to an Ashington businessman, Jack Rodway was his name
He charged a tanner for an hoor or a haff croon for the day
But ye shud hev seen the queer things that this trolley tyun away.
Noo I seen it loaded up one day wi' mats an' beds - the lot.
An' for its croonin' glory lads - a greet big chamber pot.
An' as it torned a corner ye shud hev hord the screams.
Aye they lost their inside toilet when it smashed in smithereens.
Noo it carted pigeon baskets when the bords went ower seas.
A've seen it loaded up one day wi the hens still in their crees.
An' if ye wanted a len' on it yer name went on a list.
Oh a've seen more fights aroond that thing than at the dep'ty's kist.
Noo then when it cum te shiftin' an' ye cuddn't afford a van.
Ye borrid Jack Rodway's trolley an' ye cuddn't give a dam.
But when ye tried te pull the thing ye fair wraxed yer poor owld bones.
But we nivvor hord o' them stuck up folks that people caal the Jones.
Noo it costs a blummin' fortune te send objects te the moon
But that trolley shifted haff the Horst fer nigh on haff a croon!
An' when it comes te your last day an' Peter caals yer name
Ye will see Jack Rodway's trolley standing in the Hall of fame!

Our new home, in Sycamore Street, was only a short distance from Hawthorn Road, but it still confused Father when he came back to Ashington in 1919. He went to Hawthorn Road and was surprised to find that he no longer lived there. Eventually, however, he did manage to track us down and once again our family was united.

Now normal life could begin again, and for us Milburns, normal life meant football, because football and the Milburns of Ashington had gone together long before the outbreak of war.

Before even the start of the century.

CHAPTER TWO

It all began with my great-grandfather, Jack Milburn.

During the 1880s he played in goal for village teams in Northumberland and his passion for the game was passed on to his son, my Granddad, also called Jack.

But Granddad Milburn was not Jack to the fans. They gave him another name. To them he was Warhorse Milburn.

Village football games were a major, and usually free, form of entertainment in those times and local teams commanded a lot of support when they played. Spectators in Northumberland, where coal mining was a boom industry, were hard-living, hard-working men who judged footballers by their own, tough standards. So it says a lot for Granddad that the most apt nickname they could find for him was Warhorse. He was reckoned to be the strongest, and the most tenacious fullback to ever come out of the county. Sometimes when his team ran on to the local common ground football pitch in their flannel workshirts and fustian shorts, Warhorse had come straight from the pit after a gruelling shift underground.

No miner in those hard, hungry times could afford to miss a shift, even on a Saturday morning, and Warhorse was no exception. But neither would he miss his Saturday afternoon game of football at any price. It was a punishing routine, but Granddad had a strong body and an even stronger will driving it. Somehow, he could find energy where, by rights, there should have been none and still manage to give a full ninety minutes of all-out effort to his game.

Warhorse died when I was small and the only memory I have of him is of once sitting on his knee and staring hard at a blue scar on the bridge of his nose. I was fascinated by it, but too young to understand that this was the traditional mark of his trade. Most miners have blue scars. They are caused by coal dust becoming

Warhorse Milburn (Back row, second from the right) and team-mates.

ingrained in a fresh wound. Granddad got his pitman's 'tattoo' when an explosive charge, which he had been laying underground, went off before expected.

Warhorse was one of a hardy breed of pit workers known as 'sinkers'. These were the men who opened up new pits by digging and blasting shafts which provided routes to coal seams hundreds of feet below ground.

Their skills were in big demand in South East Northumberland during the mid to late 1800s when many new mines were being sunk. Before 1850, Ashington, seventeen miles north of Newcastle, had been just a handful of farmhouses in a quiet corner of Northumberland. Its population had always hovered around the 80 mark. But with the birth of the steam age, Ashington was transformed.

The 'Great Coal Rush' arrived with a vengeance and Ashington, sitting on top of a rich harvest of the stuff, became a frontier town in the rush to exploit the 'black diamond' harvest. In 1847 the first lease was granted for the sinking of a mine in the Felham Down area of what grew to become Ashington village. Our Northumbrian dialect freely translated that into Fell-Em-Doon and although the last pit in Ashington closed in March 1988, the name still lives on through a working men's club called the Fell-Em-Doon, which stands close to the site of the original colliery.

The town's first street was a group of six colliery houses built in the pit yard. They were very basic dwellings, basic even down to their name. The street was called Six Houses!

The town grew in a network of colliery streets spreading outwards from the pityard. But the naming of the new streets continued to be strictly functional. They were First Row, Second Row, Third Row, all the way up to Eleventh Row.

The colliery rows were built quickly in blocks of 26. They stood back-to-back in long, parallel lines, occasionally intersected by streets with names like Long Row, Cross Row, and Middle Row.

At first, drinking water for the infant Ashington came from the pit along a wooden chute near the junction of a road to the nearby village of Ellington. The same junction was a gathering point in those days for travelling entertainers. Gypsies and peddlers also came to the doors of the workers' homes selling all manner of things, including a kind of watery ale called 'Swanky' which cost a penny a pail.

Warhorse and his wife, Bess, lived at number 14 Ninth Row. Although I have only a dim memory of my Granddad, I remember my Granny Bess much better. I was a teenager when she died and can recall her clearly to this day. Granny Bess was quite a character. She smoked a clay pipe and liked her beer - and couldn't care a fig who knew it! Often, when I came across her scrubbing the floor of her colliery house, a cannister of ale stood beside her bucket of water and as regularly as she dipped into one, she swigged from the other.

Her home in Ninth Row was only yards away from the Portland Hotel, originally one of two temperance hotels in Ashington. The Portland was named after the Duke of Portland, who owned much of the land in the area. Until very recently there were only three pubs in the town; not a lot for a community whose population grew to more than 30,000. However it didn't take Ashington's thirsty miners very long to find a way around the problem. They simply took over local houses or shops and formed private clubs. Beer was bought in bulk and barrels installed in each house. Members of the clubs were issued with a key with which to let themselves in, so they became known as 'Key Clubs'. To be fair, I should make it clear that these were not just drinking dens, they were social centres in the true meaning of the words and offered followers of all sorts of hobbies, from gardening to whippet racing, singing to quoit playing, somewhere to meet and indulge their harmless pastimes.

Eventually the Portland Hotel was forced by public demand to forsake its temperance ideals and become a public house. That new role was convenient for Granny who then only needed to send one of her sons across Station Road to the Portland to fetch her beer.

I loved my old Granny Milburn, partly because she didn't give a damn about what other people thought of her pipe smoking and beer drinking – and partly for Fridays. When I reached my teens, I got a job as a newspaper girl delivering copies of the Morpeth Herald, which came out on a Friday. Granny's house was on my route from Jimmy Chrisp's newsagency shop and she always had freshly baked stottie waiting for me when I called in. Stottie is a traditional North Eastern bread which is at its best when it has been cooked in a coal-fired oven. On icy winter days I always knew that when I called at Granny's house I would be handed a steaming slice of stottie straight from the oven and coated with fast-melting butter. Clutching the hot stottie in my numb fingers, I usually curled up on her wooden settle seat in a warm alcove next to her roaring coal fire to thaw out while Granny puffed at a white clay pipe, stained brown with nicotine.

Granddad never took alcohol and he didn't approve of Granny drinking, but he never managed to stop her. She reckoned her life was hard enough anyway without being denied one of her few pleasures.

As new pit shafts were sunk, Bothal(1867), Carl(1875),

Duke(1885), followed by a succession of others, the town grew rapidly and within forty years its population had mushroomed to 25,000.

That still left it short of being a teeming metropolis of course, but it was still enough for Ashington to be christened 'The Biggest Pit Village in the World'.

Warhorse and Bess made their own considerable contribution to that population boom. Granddad didn't use up all of his considerable energy on work and soccerplay. He still had enough left over for him to father his own football team plus two reserves. He and Bess had thirteen children, seven girls, five boys and one of them was my father, Tanner Milburn.

Although he was christened Jack, my father (Faatha) was known from the outset as 'Tanner', a nickname which stayed with him for the rest of his life. When Father was born, he was just half the size of his older brother Bob. So he was nicknamed Tanner - slang for sixpence, or to put it another way, half a bob! (A 'bob' was a shilling in those pre-decimalisation days)

As well as Bob and Tanner, Warhorse and Bess had my uncles Buck, Alec, Jimmy and Sam. They also had my aunts Cissie, Maggie, Florrie, Molly, Phyllis and two others whose names I don't know because they died when they were very young. The boys all inherited the Milburn flair for football. One of them, my uncle Alec, was invited to play for Tottenham Hotspur, but he had just married and his bride, Nancy, persuaded him to stay put, which was just as well for the North East. If he had not listened to her, the region would have been deprived, a generation later, of one of its all-time soccer heroes – Alec's son, and my cousin, Jackie Milburn.

Uncle Alec stayed, however, and 'Wor' Jackie, as his son became to thousands of fans, went on to earn his own special place in footballing history as centre-forward with Newcastle United and England.

My father was an accomplished footballer in his own right. He played in goal for Ashington FC when the team was a Third Division North side. He and my mother had four sons and three daughters. I was the first girl on the scene, after my brothers Jack and George.

All the boys, Jack, George, Jimmy and Stan followed what had by then become a well-established Milburn family tradition and set out to make their fortune with their feet. They all joined league football clubs and, in true Warhorse fashion, became fullbacks. Three of them, Jack, George and Jim played for Leeds United, where my own son Jack made his mark as a tough and controversial defender a generation later. Stan, the youngest of my brothers, joined Chesterfield and went on to play for Leicester City and Rochdale. Leeds' goalkeeper Jimmy Potts also took out honorary membership of the Milburn clan as an in-law, when his sister married my brother Jack.

This, then, was the clan into which I was born on 11 November 1912. I was the latest limb of a family tree whose roots were already three generations deep in football lore.

Much had already been achieved by the footballing Milburns and more was still to come. But that is only half of my family story.

My mother was born a Charlton and married a Milburn. I was born a Milburn and married a Charlton. That is not as much a coincidence as it may seem, for in the border country between England and Scotland, both names are common – and usually linked with reivers who raided villages on either side of the border for cattle or sheep!

The boom in the coal industry gave the more honest members of both clans the chance of a different way of life. Among them was my grandfather, George Charlton. He was a big, strapping man, well-known in his day as a fine morris dancer. If football was my inheritance from the Milburns then dancing was my Charlton legacy.

Granddad Charlton took his hobby very seriously. Although he was a big, tough man doing a very masculine job, he never saw anything unmanly about skipping and whooping his way through those traditional dances.

His other great love was quoits. He had his own set of steel quoits which he polished lovingly until they sparkled and whenever he set off for a quoit contest he always carefully packed the shining rings in a clean, bright red handkerchief.

Many of the competitions were held at pubs or clubs in the area. If the contest was in Ashington then it was usually at the working men's social clubs which were still multiplying through the town.

For many years Granddad Charlton enjoyed going to clubs and pubs, not for the drink, but for the opportunities they offered him to enjoy his first loves of quoits or dancing. He was never a big drinker, until one day when an argument with a policeman changed his life.

Granddad's team had won a morris dancing competition in West Northumberland and they celebrated their success with a few drinks. Afterwards Granddad was found asleep in a hedge by a passing policeman. Possibly mistaking him for a tramp, the policeman woke Granddad and ordered him to clear off.

As I mentioned earlier, Granddad was a big, strong man and he didn't take kindly to being pushed about by anyone, especially after a rude awakening. The policeman was in no mood for mincing words either and he drew his truncheon. He hit Granddad hard over the head a few times before taking him to the local lock-up. After that beating and being locked up, Granddad Charlton became a different man. He went into a mental home for a while and when he came out he began to drink heavily, something he had never done before. To make it worse, every time he got drunk he went berserk. He also developed a disturbing habit of standing in his back street late at night preaching to the moon and stars at the top of his powerful voice.

Soon his neighbours in Sycamore Street began to lock their doors when they heard his bellowing. In those days, when people just didn't bother to lock their doors, the sound of all those bolts going in against him drove him wild. Unfortunately it was his wife who took the brunt of his wrath when he had what we called 'the blue devils'. Her only option then was to pull a shawl over her shoulders and take refuge in our house, on the opposite side of the street for a few days, until he had cooled down.

It was a great shame because when he was sober there wasn't a nicer old man than my Granddad Charlton. He delighted us kids with his wicked sense of humour. One of his favourite tricks involved Granny's precious rocking chair. She was very houseproud, particularly where her furniture was concerned. Children weren't even allowed to eat at her table. If we were given a piece of bread, she lowered the coal oven door for us to use as a table. Even that had to be covered with a sheet of paper to catch any crumbs which could then be flicked into the fire. And as for that rocking chair – well, it was territory totally forbidden to us.

Her finnicky ways annoyed Granddad and he had his own way of getting even. If he was in a mood for devilment when any of his grandbairns were there, he would send Granny to Walter Willson's shop on the corner to buy him some pipe tobacco, then, the moment she was gone, he said: 'Come on', and waved us into the rocking chair. For the few minutes that Granny was away we rocked furiously while he kept look-out at the window. When she did come back she would find us waiting innocently and Granddad choking back his laughter.

I loved Granddad Charlton because he was always doing things like that. A grand old man, he had an imposing moustache, regularly waxed with Icilma cream and I thought there was no finer smell than the sweet odour of that cream. He always wore double-breasted suits and his style of dressing, combined with that greased moustache and his impressive manner made him look more like a sea captain than the pitman he was.

It's just a pity that he got drunk. He was so big and such a powerful man that people were terrified of him. It was even worse if he came across a policeman after a drinking session. Because of that beating with the truncheon, he hated the police and every time he got drunk he never missed a chance to try to get his own back. The result, of course, was that he was always being summonsed. Granny used to say that he would get a summons even if they had just heard Granddad Charlton shouting in the distance.

Small, dark and attractive, but with no sense of humour, Granny liked to wear black alpaca skirts and a belt with an ornate buckle around her slim waist. When she was dressed up in her best, with her high buttoned lace collar, rings and earrings, she was beautiful. She had once been a Sunday school teacher, which made me hold her in even greater awe. In those days, any kind of teacher commanded open-mouthed respect from us children.

My Granny overlooked a lot of Granddad's ways because until the time he was beaten he had been a good-living man who worked hard at the pit for his family and was happy to spend his free time on harmless hobbies.

He was, however, a jealous man. Once, a door-to-door salesman brought a case of clocks to their house when Granny was in on her own. He was near the end of his working day and, because he planned to pick up his round the next day where he had left off, he asked Granny if he could leave his heavy sample case at her house overnight instead of having to carry it home, then bring it back again. Granny agreed, but Granddad didn't like the arrangement. He had a typically sardonic way of showing his displeasure. Granddad opened a window and hurled the case out, then turned to Granny with a wry grin and remarked: 'My, how the time does fly!'

CHAPTER THREE

Time flew for me too after we made that move from our little flat in Hawthorn Road to the house in Sycamore Street which became our home for the next six years.

The house, built and owned by Ashington Coal Company, was certainly a step forward for us compared to our old rented flat, but looking back on it now, it was still pretty primitive. We did gain two upstairs bedrooms, one for the boys and another for the girls. But downstairs there was just one room, a combined living-room-cum-kitchen and in one corner of it, under the staircase, was the bed where Mother and Father had to sleep. A door in the room led to a walk-in pantry with the house's only supply of water - from a cold water tap. But at least the supply was indoors. In the pit rows at what we called the 'top end' of Ashington, where the first houses had been built, water still came from stand pipes in the street. The family wash was done in that pantry, but cooking was carried out on the main room's combined fire and coal oven range. That big range dominated the room. In the middle of it was a fireplace large enough to swallow coal by the bucketful. Attached to the side wall of the fireplace was a wrought iron hob which could be swiveled over the burning coals. Most of the time a big, black, steaming kettle rested on the hob. To the left of the fire was an oven heated by the fire and to the right a small set pot behind a circular cast-iron door. One of my jobs was to clean that fireplace and in those days that was a major task. For a start the fireplace looked like a celebration of the smithy's arts. Steel, brass and cast-iron everywhere; fenders and fire-irons were fashioned into intricate, twisting and filigreed shapes; beautiful now that I look back on them, but at the time they were my hated enemies. All they meant to me in those days was hard work.

The steel fender had to be polished until it shone. Brasso and elbow-grease had the brass rail over the fire gleaming like gold

To go to the toilet meant 'gannin' ower the road' to the ash midden netty seen in the centre of the picture.

Next to the netty was the coal-house. Free coal supplied by the coal company was delivered every two weeks by horse-drawn tubs and dumped outside. I hated the sight of those trucks because another one of my jobs was to shovel the coal into the coal-house.

and even the cast-iron oven and fire-grate were black-leaded until they looked like burnished ebony. Nothing less would satisfy Mother – unluckily for me.

Outside our home, we had a small yard enclosed by a short wooden fence and beyond that was the back lane. Here again, just like Hawthorn Road, it was an unmade street, rutted and uneven in the cold winter months, dusty in the dry summer months and a clarty mess when it rained. Even so, that road still had to be crossed many times every day, because on the other side of it were our middens and coal sheds.

We didn't talk of 'going to the lavatory'. We always said we were 'going over the road', or to be more accurate 'gannin ower the road'. Our outhouses were separated by an alleyway from a similar row serving homes in Pont Street, which ran parallel to our street. In front of the outhouses was a narrow gauge railway line.

Ashington's pit streets were designed in long, uniform rows with this track system in mind. Along that two-foot wide steel road, four tubs each with 15 hundredweight of coal on board, were hauled, usually by Clydesdale horses, between the coal company's central supply depot and miners' homes.

As well as deliveries of fuel, the track was also used by refuse wagons which took away the contents of our middens. It was an unpleasant job carried out by what we called 'the midden men'. Luckily for our noses it was a service performed at the dead of night when there were fewer people around to offend. Eventually this barely sanitary arrangement was scrapped and flush toilets installed - not a minute too soon. Fevers were frequent in those days and although I managed to avoid the worst of them, one smallpox epidemic put my mother and younger sister Esther in hospital. They were taken by horse-drawn ambulance to Pity Me isolation hospital half-way between Ashington and the neighbouring village of North Seaton.

I was just ten years old at the time. But that still made me the oldest female in the household. As a result it was taken for granted that I was responsible for all of Mother's chores.

Ten years old and running a house! I had only started school four years earlier, yet I did it. I had to, there was no-one else; certainly not my father and brothers. In those days housework was most definitely woman's work and the thought of helping out never even entered their heads.

Our house was put out of bounds. A large red warning notice was stuck to the front and back doors saying 'No visitors allowed'. We remained prisoners in our own home until the whole place could be fumigated – a horrible experience. The smell lingered for days and the memory of it makes me shudder yet.

I did my best to copy the jobs I had seen Mother doing, washing, cooking, cleaning, looking after the men of the house. But oh how I ached to have her back home again.

In those days bread was baked in the home and it was one of the first cookery lessons Mother taught me. Each week we had two stones of flour delivered to the house by Brough's travelling grocer. Orders collected by the grocery girl were delivered by flat-cart on the following Thursday or Friday. Until I had mastered bread-making, I always took a dish of flour to Mother and she checked that I had the correct measures of flour, salt, yeast and water before I began the arm-aching business of kneading the mixture. But as for cooking a proper dinner for Father and my big brothers, Jack and George, when they all came in from pit; the very thought terrified me. All the same, I felt I was under an obligation to make them a dinner.

Although I was overwhelmed at being put in charge of the household at that tender age, I took it for granted, as much as everyone else, that it was my duty. So I determined that I would meet my responsibilities in full and cook that proper dinner, complete with real Yorkshire puddings, for the men in my care.

I cooked the meat, prepared and boiled the vegetables, then set to work on the Yorkshire pudding mixture, bringing together the flour, eggs and milk in the same quantities which I had seen Mother use so many times before. I was so determined to get it right and so proud of the end result which I set before the men when they came in from work that night. At the end of the meal I was overjoyed to see that their plates had been cleared. But later I learned that my brothers had in fact smuggled the Yorkshire puddings outside, pushed out the middles and imitated their grandfather Charlton by playing a game of quoits with them along the midden track!

As the six long weeks which Mother spent in the fever hospital dragged by, I discovered just what a punishing amount of work she and every other pitman's wife was expected to do. As well as keeping the house tidy and clean, shopping, possing the family washing and preparing meals, I had to look after my baby brother Jimmy, who was also on the scene by then.

There was one chore I particularly hated. Every day Father, Jack and George came in from the pit with their workwear caked in dried mud and slime and it was my job to make them fit to wear for another shift. First I brushed the clothes with a stiff-bristled broom to remove the worst of the muck. Then their pit clothes, three sets of coarse flannel shirts and thick fustian pants, had to

A hewer (George Ledgerwood) at Linton Colliery in 1921, working at the coal-face. A filthy job, and one I knew well as I had to clean three sets of pit clothes every day for Father and my two brothers.

38

be hung over the oven door to dry. Because that left them rough and stiff, my next job was to rub the clothes for as long as my aching arms would allow until they were soft enough for the men to wear. It was gruelling, but something which had to be done every day and it never occurred to me to question my lot. I was used to the hard work, as were most pitmen's wives and daughters in those days.

I don't suppose it did me much harm, but it does upset me now, that women in those days were regarded as little more than slaves with no right to expect any other life. What's worse, is the fact that so many of us just accepted this cruel belief.

I also have little doubt now that this exhausting domestic slavery helped to send my mother to an early grave. Mother was dark-haired, pale and slim. A nice looking woman with an even nicer nature which my father took terrible advantage of. He wasn't any worse than other men of his generation, in the way he regarded her, but in those days men took it for granted that they would be wet-nursed by their women.

I can clearly remember Mother cooking leek puddings for him at two o'clock in the morning and thinking nothing of it. Her working day had to revolve around his working hours and because she was married to a miner that meant she also had to work shifts. When Father was on fore-shift coming home at eight a.m., he expected a full dinner to be cooked and waiting for him. It always was, but to have it ready in time for him getting home, Mother had to rise at six a.m. to light the fire which heated the coal oven before she could cook his breakfast-time dinner.

When I look back now it is little wonder that Mother's heart gave out early. She had a hard struggle, made no easier by giving birth to seven children. Each new arrival took a heavy toll on her health and she came to depend on me more and more as it got worse. I did what I could to help her. But to be truthful it was not from any sense of compassion. I was just a child with only a child's understanding of duty. I helped because I was made to help. But oh how I wept when I had to work in the house while all my friends were outside playing in the street or off to the penny matinee at the pictures.

Mother was sorry, but there was nothing she could do about it. She was so fastidious and the house had to be kept to her high standard by someone. Unfortunately that someone was me.

As I said before, there was little chance of Tanner helping with the housework. As far as he was concerned a woman's place was in the home. But I do remember one day when Tanner said he was going to the races and Mother announced that she was going with him. She was pregnant with my other sister Gladys at the time and Father decided that he didn't want Mother tagging along. But rather than make an excuse or argue his case, he just grabbed her long skirt and before she could stop him, fed it into a kitchen mangle. Ignoring both her protests and her threats he wound the rollers and her skirt was drawn in until she was completely trapped. Neighbours from across the road heard her cries for help and eventually released her, but by then Father was well clear and on his way to the races alone.

When I could steal time from my household duties the back lane was my playground. I ran, I skipped, I whipped wooden tops, played marbles, kicked pig's bladder footballs and 'coined the gurd' – a North East term for bowling an iron hoop with a stick. In the back street I also learned one of my favourite games –'Kitty Cat'.

The same game is popular in other parts of the country under a lot of different names and for some reason has its biggest following in mining villages and towns. We played 'Kitty Cat' with a small piece of shaped wood and a crude wooden bat. The wood is placed on the ground then slapped hard with the bat. As the wood springs into the air it is given a hefty whack and the winner is the player who can hit it the furthest.

Although I was as rough and tumble a tomboy as ever there was, I always refused to play one favourite boys' pastime.The game required a tin can, wet paper and carbide powder. The powder was easy enough to find. It was used to fuel miners' cap-lamps and every pitman had some of the stuff at home. Carbide powder is stable as long as it is kept dry, but once it is wet it gives off a highly flammable gas.

The game which the young tearaways of my day invented

involved pouring carbide powder into a tin and adding a few drops of water before jamming the lid back on. The sensible tearaways ran like mad because when that tin was burst open by the expanding gas inside, it went off with a tremendous bang. But not all of them were that sensible and some dreamed up even more dangerous versions of the same game. Carbide 'bombs' were dropped down drains to produce a thunderclap which rattled windows in the street. Others were thrown into manholes to see how high they could blast the cast-iron covers into the air. But the worst trick of all, which always ended in threats of the most horrible punishment for the guilty parties, involved dropping a carbide blaster into a midden. I'll leave you to imagine what resulted from that!

I preferred far more ladylike pastimes, such as stewing worms and rubbing the juice on my legs.

Let me explain. Three doors down the street from our house lived Eliza Smith, a lass two or three years older than I was. Those few years she had over me counted for a lot to my young eyes. She was a fountain of knowledge on the matter of dancing as far as I was concerned and one day when she announced that she was going to choreograph a street concert and invited me to be part of it, I jumped at the chance. Along with some of the other girls in the street, I began to go to 'rehearsals' at Eliza's house twice a week when her mother went out to the pictures. We worked hard under Eliza's direction, practising our steps and graceful hand movements. We managed the chorus parts and the more supple ones did crabs and handstands, but the one thing no-one could manage was the splits. No matter how hard we tried, we just couldn't stretch our aching muscles any further.

Then Eliza announced that she knew of a special potion which would loosen our muscles just enough for us to do the splits.

'Get some worms and stew them in the oven,' she commanded. We obeyed without question because Eliza knew so much about dancing.

'The fatter they are, the more juice there'll be from them,' she added as we left for our gardens.

We dug up a handful of the fattest, slimiest worms we could

find and marched back to Eliza with our catch. The worms, in a tin lid, were shoved into the coal oven at Eliza's home and stewed for the recommended time. Once they had cooled, we rubbed the revolting mixture into the backs of our legs and guess what? It stiffened them up!

We never did manage to do the splits, but we still carried on with our rehearsals and still staged the concert without any more of Eliza's exotic potions.

CHAPTER FOUR

I started the South School, a big, red-bricked Edwardian building at the bottom of Sycamore Street, when I was six years old and left when I reached the grand age of fourteen. I could have gone on to a high school in nearby Newbiggin - I had passed my scholarship exam and was entitled - but I was a girl and one of a family of seven. As far as Mother and Father were concerned, any money they spent to educate me further would be money wasted, particularly in the year that I reached school leaving age.

It was 1926, the year of the general strike, and a time of hardship for miners and their families. Eventually the fight was lost and the miners were forced to go back to work on the pit owners' terms. But before then we all had to learn some hard lessons in survival. We discovered – because we had to – how to stretch the pennies, eke out the dwindling coal supply and how to eat when there seemed to be no food.

Debts which built up in pit communities like my own during that bitter dispute, were a millstone which some people had to bear for decades afterwards. So it came as no great surprise that when I reached fourteen there was no question of the family's limited funds being spent on educating me any more. I had no option but to leave school.

I was sad and disappointed when my schooldays came to an end, I had loved them, not so much for the lessons, but because school was my escape from a seemingly endless list of household chores which Mother always had ready for me. In spite of the strict discipline exercised by my teachers, school was still a kind of freedom for me. It was also somewhere for me to put my own share of the Milburn talent for sport to good use. Soon after starting school I set myself a goal; I was going to be captain of the South School's netball team and nothing would stop me. Every player on the team got a uniform consisting of a brown gymslip, brown knickers and, if you could make captain, a yellow girdle. I wanted that yellow girdle desperately and in the end I got it. I allowed nothing and no one to stand between me and that dream, not even my brothers although they did their best to put me off. It was terrible if they discovered when my team had a match to play. When they did find out, they turned up on the touchline and heckled me mercilessly. 'Howay Skinny Liz,' and 'Show us yer knickers Tin Ribs,' they yelled – I could have killed them!

In the end I pleaded with Mother to spare my blushes and not let the boys know when I had a game coming up.

I loved sport at school, although the only games on offer were netball for the girls and football for the boys. There was no provision for budding athletes then; no encouragement at all of the sort that pupils with any kind of ability for sport are given today. I just wish there had been the same chance in my day. Given that kind of opportunity, I'm sure that I could have been a top class athlete myself. But the only chance we had to show our field event skills was at Ashington's Annual Sports Day.

Once a year, all of the town's children assembled at their schools on a Saturday and marched in parade to People's Park at the 'top end'. At the park entrance gates each of us was given a penny and a bag of sweets paid for by the town's miners. For months leading up to the big day, the money which paid for it had been deducted in small amounts from the miners' wage packets. The cash also provided a half-crown voucher for each event-winner, which could only be exchanged for goods at Paddy Mullen's haberdashery shop just off Station Bridge in Ashington town centre.

All of us Milburns were regularly among the winners at these sports days and – annually speaking – we were among Paddy Mullen's regulars. I usually bought a new pinnie and it became the one item of new clothing I could rely on having every twelve-month.

The boys were as strong and fit as Father could make them and when they trained I trained with them. No allowances were made for the fact that I was a girl, nor did I expect any, not even when it came to bareknuckle boxing! One of my brothers' favourite en-

44

Station Bridge in Ashington before the First World War. We were regular visitors to Paddy Mullen's shop after Ashington's Annual Sports Day.

tertainments was to watch my sister Etty and me boxing and the big event was taken very seriously.

Just picture the scene if you will – here we are then, ready for the main event – a bruising battle between the Sycamore Street sisters, Cis and Etty Milburn. My brothers have cleared all the furniture from the centre of the living-room and strung Mother's clothesline between four chairs, each forming a corner of a make-shift boxing ring.

Etty and me climb over the rope with the lads already shouting their encouragement.

Seconds out and we leap at each other, fists flying. Thump! Wallop! Smack! We belt the daylights out of each other until one of us is declared the winner.

Of course we didn't do it entirely for the boys' entertainment. We insisted that there had to be a prize purse to compensate for our bumps and bruises. Usually the lads coughed up sixpence for the winner which was just enough to buy new pair of stockings. Many's the time I earned a pair of stockings that way – and a black eye to boot!

Although I loved sport when I was at school, I wasn't a duffer at the academic subjects. What I didn't like were the domestic subjects. They were too much like the chores waiting for me at home.

I liked them even less when my outspoken manner landed me in trouble with my cookery teacher, Miss Simpson. As Christmas 1925 approached, she announced that we would all be making Christmas presents for her. That just didn't seem right or fair to me. If I was going to make Christmas presents for anyone it should be for my family or friends. Unfortunately for me this was another of those times when I just had to speak my mind.

I was dawdling as I worked on a pouffe for Miss Simpson and she could see that I was not very enthusiastic about my work. She asked sharply: 'Don't you want to do that?' Maybe another time I would have mildly answered, 'Yes Miss'. But my fins were already up at the unfairness of having to make it at all and her sharp manner was the last straw.

I shouted, 'No I don't want to do it.' and told her why.

I was made to regret that outburst for the remainder of my schooldays. From that moment she gave me a terrible time during her lessons: if there was a rotten job to be done, such as scrubbing out dirty cupboards, I was given it. I suppose she was just doing her job by being seen to put me in my place, but I didn't see it that way at the time.

One strict rule at the school was that boys and girls had to be kept apart. As a result we had separate teachers, classrooms, and playgrounds. A high, red-brick wall with a stout wooden gate divided the playground with boys on one side and girls on the other and heaven help anyone found on the wrong side without a very good reason - which was a pity, because on the other side of that wall, at the boys' end, was a round-faced lad with a Cheshire Cat grin and a flair for poaching. A lad who, seven years and two broken engagements later, became my husband, Bob Charlton.

In spite of all the obstacles, however, the boys and girls still met up. At night, after school, I kept my ears cocked for the sound of someone whistling 'Moonlight and Roses' in the lane outside.

It was whistled by a bunch of boys sauntering down my street as a signal to us girls that they would be waiting outside the South School at the bottom end of Sycamore Street.

Of course mothers aren't as daft as their daughters would like them to be and usually had a ruse of their own to deal with the situation. My mother always insisted that if I was going out I had to take my young brother, Jimmy, with me in his pushchair. My protests at the injustice and indignity of it all fell on deaf ears; my only consolation was that as I heaved Jimmy and his pushchair out of our back yard, my best friend, Bessie Glenton, in Pont Street, the opposite pit row, was usually doing the same with her baby brother Ronnie. Her mother, like mine, knew the value of a chaperone in nappies. Not that either of them had any real need to worry; we were so very innocent in those days, the boys as well as the girls.

In my early teen years I also discovered my second great love (second to football) – dancing. Father didn't like me going to the local dances, but I never let that put me off. I came to an arrangement with my brother Jack to get around Father's objection. Jack didn't enjoy dancing, but was a firm film fan. So we reached a pact that we would tell Father that I had been to the pictures with Jack although, in fact, we went our separate ways as soon as we were able. I headed for the nearest dance hall, at North Seaton Miner's Welfare Hall, a mile from our home. First, however, I studied the still photographs outside the cinema to get an idea of the story and the film's stars in case Father questioned me afterwards. It is laughable now, but remember, we were barely out of Victorian times in those days.

There was one way which I could enjoy dancing with Father's approval and that came by courtesy of our next-door neighbour, Mr Taylor. Mr Taylor played the accordian and he had a fiddle-playing friend who often came round to his house where they would accompany each other in making music which even now, almost seventy years afterwards, I can still recall vividly.

Picture, as I can now, a hot summer night. The two friends are in our dusty back lane sitting on little wooden stools called crackets. There is no-one else about as Mr Taylor squeezes out the opening notes of a popular catchy Northumbrian reel which is picked up by the fiddle.

At first they are playing for their own amusement, but as soon as we children hear the sound of their jolly music we run outside to gather around them and listen. The lane gradually fills, first with their music, then with the excited chatter of us youngsters. The grown ups come out and while some settle for tapping their toes, others begin to dance, whipping up little clouds of dust as they skip and spin. The excitement they create with their music is contagious. It lasts through that long summer night and for those dancing hours the men can forget the horror of working below ground and the women can forget their domestic slavery.

Putting it bluntly, Tanner, was a rogue. He gambled, he drank and he wasn't above juggling the odds or bending the law to make himself an extra bob or two. Those people who can still recall him remember a quick-witted character with a cocky kiss-curl and an open hand when he was on a winning streak. But that was his public face. In private he could be a very different man. Don't get me wrong, I'm not saying that he was ever physically violent to Mother or us kids. But he was a very selfish man. As a child I never really noticed. But looking back now I see that his penny-pinching ways amounted to a kind of cruelty which added one more burden to my mother's already hard life. He also provoked my brother Stan into abandoning a promising future in athletics. But more about that later.

Although Father would happily go on a drinking spree buying rounds for his cronies at the social club when he'd had a win on the horses or the dogs, he was a different man at home where every penny had to be accounted for. He never overlooked a domestic debt. If Mother borrowed a shilling from him it had to be paid back to the last farthing. He didn't have it all his own way, however.

Mother, quiet as she was, had her own special way of parting Tanner from his cash. Whenever we kids needed clothes we were marched up to the Constitutional social club in North Seaton Road. She knew that Father would be inside, but wouldn't go in after him. Instead she waited outside until he came out just after

48

My dad, Tanner Milburn, or Prisoner of War Number 1749, as he was when this photograph was taken.

three o'clock. When he did put in an appearance, Mother would demand a share of his winnings in full view and hearing of his drinking pals, then make him take us all to the town-centre shops nearby to separate him from some of his cash. Embarrassed at being put on the spot and addled by the drink, he was little match for Mother in full righteous flight and usually did little more than cough up.

Father was a miner by trade, a bookie's runner by inclination and a sportsman by instinct. I first became part of his shady gambling operation when I was still a small girl – he made me one of his own runners. Everyone knew that Father was a bookie's runner, including, I am sure, the police. But knowing and proving are two very different things. Father's 'pitch' from where he usually collected bets for a bookie, was at a corner-end on Milburn Road, near our house, in Sycamore Street. There was no law against just standing there passing the time of day with whoever happened to walk by and that is what the casual observer would see. Sometimes they would even see Tanner's daughter, Little Cis, arrive, toy tin bucket in hand and exchange a few words before skipping away. But the closer observer would have seen slips of paper and money in that little bucket.

Punters often brought their bets to our house and if Father was out, Mother would put the bets in that little seaside bucket of mine and send me straight off to find him. Usually I found him in time at the corner-end and my reward as his runner was a halfpenny ice-cream bought from Mr Notriani's gaily decorated push-cart.

Running bets was, of course, strictly illegal but Father was too fly to let himself be caught by the police. He was also too fast. He was a very athletic man, 5ft 8in tall, thin but extremely fit. He played in goal for Ashington during the days when the team was a Third Division side and he was said to be the best left-handed goalie in the business.

During those years between the wars, all kinds of sports flourished in Ashington. Most of the men in the town earned a living by tough physical graft and as a rule were very fit. Sport was also encouraged by employers who presumably saw it as a better use of free time than swilling beer, and religious groups who were equally anxious to promote 'healthy' pursuits. As early as 1866 a recreation ground (we called it The Rec) was flourishing in the shadow of Fell-Em-Doon pit. Its users soon had a choice of cricket, football, rugby, hockey, wrestling and cycle racing and the annual sports day became a mecca for thousands of spectators. Over the years, as the town grew, other sports areas came into being.

Portland Park became home for the town's football team called (what else) The Colliers. Another large welfare ground was developed to serve the Hirst area of Ashington, a cricket club was established in the town centre and a number of parks and fields throughout provided unofficial sports areas.

As well as footballers, Ashington also produced some fine sprinters, some of them trained by my father. Many sprinters with their sights set on the Powderhall Handicap, the Morpeth Olympics or one of the many other professional foot race events which were so popular in those days, came to Father for special coaching. His expertise was also passed on to his own sons and grandsons. Before Father died he saw that his grandson Bobby Charlton had outstanding natural skill and did his best to encourage Bobby to make the most of it.

A generation earlier, when Father was training his own sons, it wasn't for entirely unselfish reasons. As far as he was concerned the time he had spent training them was an investment and he expected a dividend. He got that dividend in the way that came easiest to him – by betting. But he gambled and lost on the day he tried to sell my brother Stan short.

When I was in my late teens and early 20s, I often went with Father and my brothers to athletics meetings. Handicap races were run regularly in the area around Ashington and Morpeth. The Morpeth Olympics was the premier event for the district, with a 110-yard sprint the main race. Stan knew enough about his own strengths as well as his opponents' to be able to forecast pretty accurately the outcome of the race. This was valuable inside information for Tanner, but information he could not use without shortening the odds. He was just too well-known in the area as a gambling man with a good eye for a bet and anything or anyone backed by him was well noted by the other punters. The situation called for a decoy – and I was usually it. While Father went to the pub or just strolled around the race ground looking as if he wasn't especially interested in what was going on, I had to watch Stan closely. If he bent down and fastened his lace just before the start of the race that was my signal to run to the bookie and bet on him to win.

The arrangement worked well enough until Father went too far at a big competition in Amble. If Stan had produced too good a time before the final race he would have been handicapped. So, under strict instructions from Father, Stan did well enough in preliminary heats to qualify for a place in the final, but not well enough to attract a handicap penalty.

Stan was about eighteen and at the peak of his form at the time. He had trained hard, with Father's help, and was set to take the top prize of £20, a fantastic amount in those days.

Owing to his carefully controlled run-up performances he drew a good position in the contest. He sailed through the semi-final and it became obvious from the earlier races that Stan had only one real opponent. Just before the final race a gathering storm broke. Thunder rolled and the ground was drenched in the downpour. As Stan and his chief rival waited for the weather to clear and the race to start, Father drew the other lad's manager to one side and between them they made a deal. Father had won some money from betting on Stan's placings in the preliminary races, but he was not prepared to gamble on the outcome of the final. He decided that if the two lads were so evenly matched it was time to hedge his bet.

The deal that he struck with the other lad's manager was that whichever of the two boys won, the purse would be shared equally between the two managers. Stan knew nothing of the deal and ran to win. He threw all he had to give into breaching that tape first and was bitterly disappointed when his rival pipped him at the post. But that was nothing compared to his fury when Father told him about the deal.

In Father's book coming second deserved no reward and he decided that Stan wouldn't get a penny from his half of the prize money. He argued that it all belonged to him for having the foresight to not let family loyalty overcome his gambler's instinct.

Stan stormed off in a black rage. When we got home that night, he threw his running pumps into the fire and told Father 'You'll never do that to me again.'

He was right. Stan never did race again, although he did go on to make himself a successful career in soccer with Leicester City.

Just before I left school when I was fourteen, we moved home once again, the last time as a complete family. My older brothers, George and Jack, signed as professionals with Leeds United and left home just before the start of the 1926 General Strike. When it came, the strike hit some families quickly and soup kitchens soon had to be set up in Ashington's social clubs to feed families without the money to feed themselves. We were slightly luckier than some. Father's earnings as a bookie's runner managed to keep us going for a little while longer than most. But it only postponed the crunch: it couldn't prevent it.

I was soon in the bread line with the rest of my friends and relations. We went to the Comrades Social Club in North Seaton Road, twice a day. The first time was to collect a slice of bread and the second for a bowl of soup.

I also often went coal picking on the local pit heaps with my father. Not that we needed fires to warm our homes, for those summer weeks of the strike were among the best that I can ever remember; the weather was glorious.

We needed the coal to heat our ovens and cook the meagre meals we could get from the Co-op store with food vouchers from the 'parish'.

One day during the strike Mother was cooking some girdle scones and the smell of those hot scones had my mouth watering. Suddenly a strange man ran through our open front door and was sprinting for the back door when he skidded to a halt in front of the oven. He sniffed and said sarcastically: 'Aah see yer not se hard up ye cannit afford girdle scones.'

Mother answered: 'Aye, and aah'm not se hard up that a cannit afford te stot a few of them off yer heed.'

But she knew she wouldn't have time to pelt him because this man was on the run and he would not be there long enough for her to hit him.

It was common practise in our street to leave both doors open when the men were playing pitch and toss in Wembley field, nearby. They always posted lookouts while they illegally gambled on the toss of two coins and as soon as a policeman was spotted, the men would scatter. If a stranger unexpectedly sprinted through your home, it was a pound to a penny that there was a copper close behind, although by the time the policeman arrived, both doors were usually shut.

A lot of gambling schools operated in Wembley field, at the bottom of our street, that long summer. It was something for idle hands to do and it helped the men to forget their empty bellies and worried wives for a short while as the strike dragged on.

They were desperate days and, in spite of the work around the house which I was able to do, I felt very much that I was a non-paying 'passenger' in my family. It was obvious that I had to forget any hope of carrying on with my schooling. But neither could I stay at home much longer, adding to my parents' burden. Somehow I had to find work – but where? Even in those days work was hard to find in the North East, particularly for girls.

In the end I joined an exodus of young northern girls who went to London to 'go to place' and skivvy for the gentry or the new rich.

It was little more than slavery for many of us. But life 'downstairs' taught me a lot.

CHAPTER FIVE

I began my new life in the South by first heading for Seventh Row, in Ashington. I had been given the address of a woman there who ran a sort of jobs agency putting girls like me in touch with prospective employers looking for domestic workers. We called such jobs 'going to place'.

Not long aftewards I was told that a 'place' had been found for me. I was terrified because I was only fourteen and my life until then had been spent in a close-knit mining village. Now I was about to take a strange job with strange people in a strange city. I didn't want to go, but I couldn't stay in Ashington.

It must have been hard on my mother as well. I had been her right-hand helper over the years and her health was getting worse. As I boarded the eight p.m. London-bound bus her words of warning about white slavers and not talking to strangers were still ringing in my ears; as if I wasn't worried enough already!

In my pocket were directions to a Watford address and ahead of me a twelve hour journey. My employer turned out to be a man called Fowler. He was one of two brothers, who owned a jam factory. Elsie Wright, another Ashington lass who had 'gone to place', was already working for one of the brothers and I went to the other one. His home was in Rickmansworth Road, Watford and I was employed there as a 'general maid', which was just another way of saying 'skivvy'.

When I arrived in London I was met by Mr Fowler's wife and she took me straight to their house. Having come straight from a colliery row, Mrs Fowler's home seemed like a palace to me. The approach to it was along a drive leading to a square, red-paved patio.

I entered through the front door and found myself in an imposing, red-tiled hallway. Ahead of me were two large doors, one led to a dining-room and the other to a drawing-room. The drawing-room floor was tiled with parquet flooring and covered in sheep-skin rugs. For someone like me accustomed, as I was, to home-made 'clippie' mats made from cloth clippings poked into a length of hessian, this was unimagined luxury.

Further on was a kitchen – my kitchen. This was where I would work for the next two years. Unlike the rest of that house the kitchen and my room, just off it, was cramped and far less glamorous.

I had been travelling all night, I was tired, overawed, fright-ened, homesick and thoroughly miserable. On my arrival at the Fowler home I was given my first meal there – finnan haddock – and to this day I have never been able to eat that fish without the taste bringing back the feeling of total misery which settled on me that first day in Watford.

Only the memory of my brothers' taunts kept me there. They had jeered that I would never be able to stick it in Watford and my determination to prove them wrong was all that made me stay. As it happens, it was a year later before I saw them again. My fare to London had been paid by the Fowlers, but only on condition that if I failed to work the full year for them, I would repay the fare in full.

I gritted my teeth and stuck it out for that year, but there never was a happier girl than me when that year was up and I headed North for a two week holiday. I was even glad to see my taunting brothers who were also back home for their closed season break. That fortnight with the whole family back together again passed far too quickly and when I returned to Watford the homesickness was worse than ever. Even the maid in the house next door noticed. She once said to me: 'I can always tell when you are homesick because you sing.' I sang a lot in Watford.

It took a long time to overcome my homesickness, but I never got over the shock of discovering the class system. Until I went to work 'below stairs' I had never encountered snobbery. Class was something new and it horrified me to discover people who re-garded me as being beneath them when they didn't know the first thing about me.

Why, just because I was a miner's daughter, should I and so

Sister Gladys and brother Stan outside our Laburnum Terrace home after I had 'gone to place'.

many other girls in my situation, be called 'guttersnipe'? Why should I have to bow and scrape to someone else who, as far as I could see, was no better than me? They were the lessons of socialism, but lessons I learned without being consciously aware of politics.

Hard work didn't scare me. I was well used to that. Even so, the daily grind expected of me in the Fowler household was little short of slavery. Before eight o'clock in the morning I had to have the dining-room cleaned, the drawing-room done, the fires swept out, re-made and lit. Neither was it enough to just have the hall clean: it had to be washed, dried and wiped over with milk to give its red tiles the glaze demanded by my employer. Imagine that! Using milk, just to give those tiles a shine. The hunger and poverty of the 1926 strike was still fresh in my mind and this seemed a terrible extravagance.

Having completed my early morning jobs I then had to make breakfast and take it up to Mr and Mrs Fowler and all before eight o'clock. I was a staff of one in that place and for seven days a week I had to be up with the lark to get it all done.

Of the seven days, Monday was the worst – it was washing day. In my small kitchen there was a solitary gas fire and in front of it, every Monday, I had to wash, dry and iron the whole family's clothes. It was a job I hated at any time of the year, but in the winter months it was ten times worse because clothes wouldn't dry properly and my little kitchen was permanently damp. My reward for working from morning until night, seven days a week, was just eight shillings.

I had every other Sunday and one half day a week off. But that half day didn't start until three o'clock and it was thoroughly begrudged. Mrs Fowler always tried to think up some kind of excuse to hold me back when it got near my finishing time. And woe betide me if anything was broken as I worked.

One day I did break a chamberpot and it took my whole week's wage to buy a replacement. That wasn't the worst of it. On my afternoon off I usually met up with about eight other girls who were also in service. Together we would go to a cafe for a cup of tea and a doughnut, or for a walk in the park.

Mrs Fowler wouldn't let me have time off to buy a replacement and I had to get the new chamberpot in my own time. The embarrassment of carrying that thing around with me ruined my afternoon off and still makes me blush even now. I have to admit, though, that Mrs Fowler succeeded in making her point, because I never broke another thing while I was with her.

My duties in the Fowler household kept me busy most of the time. Even so, I did manage to make a little time for football. Mr and Mrs Fowler had a son, John. He was just two years younger than me and I began to teach him to play football.

Years later I was contacted by a sheep farmer in New Zealand who asked if I was the same Elizabeth Milburn who played football with him in the garden of his Watford home when he was twelve: it was that same John Fowler from all those years ago.

I worked for the Fowler family for two years and then, when I was sixteen, I was offered another job. At the Fowlers' I had been a 'general maid', although general dogsbody would have been a better title for me. My new position was as a mother's help and that was a different proposition altogether. I worked at Harrow on the Hill for Mrs Winnie Oakley. She was a schoolteacher and her husband worked in the City. They had two small children, Janet and Raymond, and we all became firm friends. Janet was two and Raymond was just a babe in arms when I arrived. I really loved those bairns and I became more an adopted member of the family than an employee.

I wasn't Cissie Milburn to them; that was a name my family and friends up North used. To everyone in the South I was 'Betty' Milburn.

Mrs Oakley and her husband were very keen hikers and sometimes when they were away on rambles I would make a traditional Geordie treat for the travellers' return; singin' hinnies, they were called in the North East – girdle scones anywhere else. I made them as my mother had shown me years earlier in Sycamore Street and the Oakleys loved them. They showed their appreciation many times over in so many small ways which meant a lot to me. For instance my brothers Jack and George were playing for Leeds United at that time and whenever Leeds met Chelsea, Arsenal or Tottenham I was always able to take that Saturday off and go to the game.

But the one kindness shown by Mrs Oakley which stands way above the rest sounds like something out of a storybook.

I had received an invitation to an international night at a posh hotel in London. The event had been organised by Harrow

YWCA, which I had joined to make new friends and give me something to do on my days off. But that international evening put me in a real quandary. It was to be held in the Russell Hotel at Russell Square and would be a posh, evening-dress affair. But just like Cinderella, I didn't have a dress for the ball. Wages earned by mother's helps didn't stretch to evening-dresses. When I explained my problem to Mrs Oakley she told me not to worry and went calling at the house next door where three girls of about my age lived.

She asked if any of them could help and just like the best of fairy godmothers, she returned with a dress which I can picture to this day. It was pink with a tulle collar and a cape top. The girls also fitted me out with an evening bag and when I paraded in front of my bedroom mirror I thought I was Queen of the May. I met up with the other girls from the YMCA and together we caught our 'carriage' to the hotel - an open-topped London Transport bus.

Having climbed up the stairs to the most prominent seats we could find and, just in case our fancy frocks weren't catching enough attention, we broke out into song. We 'Tiptoed through the tulips' at the tops of our voices all the way to our destination.

When we arrived we were able to sample exotic foods prepared by members of the YWCA from different countries. Afterwards, we danced and, best of all, none of it disappeared at the stroke of midnight.

I treasured every minute of that evening and on the way back in the bus I decided to hold on to every memory of that night so that not a minute of it would ever escape. Not one has escaped yet.

I spent two happy years working for the Oakleys, until Dr McLean, my mother's GP wrote to tell me that he thought I should come back to look after her. He thought she had cancer and only had two years to live. But it turned out later that she did not have the disease and so, after a short spell back home at Ashington, I went in search of work again.

I found a job in Leeds. My brothers were already living there and Mother was happier knowing that I was near them.

My new job was in Dalton Avenue, near my brother Jack's house, where I worked there as a mother's help to Horace Longstaff, a wholesale vegetable merchant who had four young sons.

I enjoyed working for the family because my relationship with Mrs Longstaff was not that of mistress and maid. She was not very strict and didn't insist that I wear a maid's uniform. Happily for me I had found another home from home rather than a place of work.

Mrs Longstaff was a lovely lady and on Monday nights after I had helped her with the major task of tackling a mass of family washing, she often said to me, 'Nip up and see your Jack for five minutes and bring some fish and chips in with you when you come back.'

Mr Longstaff was a Leeds supporter. He went to the match every Saturday and I went with him. Jack and George saw that I got into the football ground and I would meet up with Mr. Longstaff afterwards to go back home.

During the two years I worked in Leeds I became engaged. My fiancé was a young boy called Charlie Burton.

Engagements in those days were more a way of declaring honourable intent than anything else and my relationship with Charlie was never very serious. After a few months we went our separate ways although fifty years later, after my husband's death, he did get in touch with me again.

Throughout my time in Leeds I suffered from throat trouble. Doctors later decided it was quinsy and that for some reason the Leeds air disagreed with me. My mother came down to see Jack and noticed that I was cleaning windows with a flannel around my throat. She took one look and told me, 'We aren't that hard-up. Come home.' So home I went.

I was really sad to leave, because in Leeds I had had my first taste of real independence and freedom.

When I came back to Ashington I got a job with pork butcher called Jack Oliver. During the week I worked in his Ashington shop, making pies and at weekends I served behind the counter at his other shop in the neighbouring seaside town of Newbiggin. My pay was the princely sum of ten shillings a week, paid, grudgingly, on Saturdays.

I didn't mind the work, apart from one thing – having to fetch

Teenage frolicking at Newbiggin in the North Sea's bitterly cold waters.
That's me second from the left.

the stuff to make the pies from a cupboard in the shop. I was
absolutely terrified in case I would find a mouse when I opened
the cupboard door.

I'd had a fear of mice since I was a bairn living in Hawthorn
Road. There were hundreds of them living in the spoil ground
outside my home and sometimes they would come into the house.
I vividly remember those times when mice did manage to get in
through a hole near the fireplace at Hawthorn Road. In spite of
being a tomboy, every time I caught sight of one I jumped onto the
kitchen table and screamed as hard as I could while mother chased
around the room whacking the floor with her shoe until she had
either squashed or chased away the little intruder.

I was so scared of coming across a mouse in the butcher s shop
that every time I went to the cupboard door I always knocked first,
not for permission to go in, but to make sure that any unwelcome
little guests had time to hide from me. Even so, there was one time
when my warning didn't work and mouse scuttled out towards
me. I was in my twenties, but like that little toddler who jumped
on the kitchen table, I screamed loud and long. I also bolted from

the shop, shot across the main street and ended up in a baker's on the other side of the road!

In the early 1930s I began to date an Ashington boy, Joe Bennett. This time I was serious when we got engaged and I was heartbroken when Joe began to date another lass and we broke up.

Then I met a lad called Bob Charlton.

CHAPTER SIX

Bob was also on the rebound when we met at The Princess dance hall in Ashington.

I had gone there hoping to cheer myself up after splitting with Joe. But I just sat against the hall wall, feeling good and sorry for myself. Then a handsome lad with a big grin came up to me. He said: 'You've fallen out with your lad and I've fallen out with my lass, let's have this dance.' We got up for a St. Bernard's waltz and suddenly I was back in love again.

Six months later we were married. But many times afterwards in the years to come I asked him, 'What did you want to marry an ugly thing like me for?' He was so good looking.

Bob was a coal cutter at Linton Colliery, two miles from Ashington and I was a pork butcher's assistant, so neither of us had much money. The days of big wages for miners were still forty years away.

We certainly couldn't afford a white wedding and got married at the nearest registry office in Morpeth. After we had gone through the formalities which made us man and wife we went back to Mam's house for the reception. She was still living at Laburnum Terrace, not having died within two years as the doctor had predicted. All the same she was still very ill and had to spend a lot of her time in bed. She was certainly not up to organising my wedding reception. That was done by my Aunt – Aunt Cissie, whose nickname I had inherited and who was always there to lend a helping hand whenever it was needed. She offered to do all the catering for my wedding reception and even bought my trousseau. Once again my 'other mother' had come to the rescue. Wedding receptions were usually held at home in those days and were much nicer because of it. An accordion player had been hired for the night and in a happy, noisy, crowd, our families and friends crammed into the big kitchen to dance and sing as we

The Princess Ballroom in Ashington where I met my Bob.

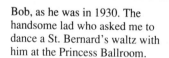

Bob, as he was in 1930. The handsome lad who asked me to dance a St. Bernard's waltz with him at the Princess Ballroom.

Bob and me on a day out.

65

celebrated the first day of a marriage which lasted the next forty nine years.

The strange thing about Bob, considering that Ashington was such a hotbed of football fanatics, was his complete lack of interest in the game. He was as bored by football as I was excited about it. Bob's sport was boxing. Many miners in those days were excellent boxers. Their difficult job below ground made many of them physically fit and mentally tough.

Travelling boxing booths provided some of these pitmen with welcome pocket money as they pitted their strength and stamina against the experience of the travelling professionals.

Apart from the organised boxing contests there were also plenty of unofficial 'bouts'. When two men had a disagreement in those days they often settled it by putting on gloves and going a few rounds in the boxing ring at the miners' welfare hall.

Every Friday night, boxing contests were held at Paddy's Market, an area of open land next to Portland Park, Ashington Football Club's home ground. Bob sometimes took me along to them. I didn't like boxing, but I would go along, especially during our courting days, just to please him. What we put up with in the name of love!

One Friday, Bob decided to chance his arm in the boxing booth ring, trading punches for a princely purse of £1 which would go to the winner. I looked on anxiously as he climbed into the ring and cheered with relief afterwards when he climbed out victorious - and £1 richer.

Bob won more than a boxing match that day. With his prize money he bought a wedding ring for me from Alexander's jewellery shop, in Station Road. It cost him 17s 6d and I wear it to this day.

The 2s 6d we had left bought us a fireplace kerb. We arranged to rent two rooms from Jean Ferrel, a local hairdresser, then took on the biggest debt either of us had known in our lives. We went into Newcastle, the nearest big city, and committed ourselves, with quite a few misgivings to £11 worth of furniture on tick. That princely sum, which seemed so much to us at the time, bought a bed, a table, a sideboard four chairs and a hearth-rug to go beside our half-a-crown fireplace kerb. I had to pay five shillings a week for those few furnishings and it worried me until the day that debt was cleared.

Neither was it my only worry. Just as we were about to move into the rooms, Jean said she needed them for a salon. We were left with no choice but to move in with Bob's mother.

Fortunately, our days of living-in didn't last too long, thanks to a little blackmail by me Mam. We had been married for two months when a flat next door to my mother's house at 18 Laburnum Terrace fell vacant. Below the flat, which was at the end of the terrace, was a shop which served as a booking office for a bus company. Staff at the shop had to share the washhouse and toilet in Mother's yard, which put her in a good position to do a bit of arm twisting.

She told the bus company bosses that if they wouldn't rent it to Bob and me they could say goodbye to the use of her lavatory. We got the flat and the bus company saved its workers from a lot of discomfort.

I couldn't work after I married because I was needed once again to look after Mother. In any case, not long afterwards, I found that I was pregnant. On the 8th May 1935 our firstborn arrived. We called him Jack. Two years later our second son arrived on the 12th of October. We christened him Robert, and called him Bobby.

Since my return from Leeds my throat trouble had never quite cleared up. In fact it had got worse as the years went by. The problem came to a head in 1938.

I had been carrying a bucketful of burning cinders downstairs after cleaning out my coal fire when everything around me began to spin. I could see the loft hatch above me and felt as if I were floating up to it. In fact I was actually tumbling down the stairs with the hot embers spilling all around me.

By a miracle I escaped being badly burned and Mother, who had heard the crash as I fell, got to me before the embers could set the flat on fire with me and the boys inside.

The doctors decided I had a thyroid problem and needed surgery. I had the operation at the Royal Victoria Infirmary in

Newcastle and afterwards I was ordered to lie flat on my hospital bed. In spite of my pleas for a backrest, I was made to stay that way for three weeks. It took a war to get me that backrest.

The year was 1939 and one of the early raids by German bombers was aimed at factories on the banks of the river Tyne. When bombs began to fall on some flour mills along the riverside, doctors decided we were just too close for comfort. But not all patients were well enough to be taken out of their wards during the raid, including me. Patients with thyroid conditions tend to be nervy and excitable at the best of times so the doctors ordered that we should be kept as calm as possible.

As I lay there listening to the 'crump' of the bombs a nurse came running up, pushed a backrest under me and thrust some wool and knitting needles into my hands.

'Knit like mad!' she commanded, and knit I did!

My thyroid operation was a success and eventually I was able to get back home to my husband, my sons, and football.

In those days my youngest brother, Stan, played for Ashington Football Club and worked at a local pit. Later he transferred to Chesterfield where our brother George was by then team coach. Later still, Stan went on to play for Leicester City and Rochdale.

I often spent my Saturday afternoons at Portland Park watching the 'Colliers' in action. Bob wouldn't come with me but he never objected to me going to games. He would even look after the kids while I went to Leeds with my father to watch Jack and George when they were playing for Leeds United. Bob was very good that way. In fact I began to suspect that he was glad to get rid of me for a bit of peace and quiet!

If I didn't have the money to go to Leeds, I went to watch the 'Colliers' or walked to the Colliery Welfare ground to see works and club teams in action. I was a football addict, whatever the level of the game.

I took Jack and Bobby with me to Ashington's home games from a very early age. Poor little Bobby, just a babe in his pram, would jump with fright at the roar whenever a goal was scored. It wasn't fair really, but he was getting fresh air and I was getting my football.

Bobby was a quiet lad then, just as he is a quiet man now. But Jack was just the opposite and has never changed either. Jack was a livewire, always getting into scrapes and usually leading other kids into trouble with him.

Trouble for Jack also usually meant trouble for me. I stood by him and made excuses and apologies of course, but I told him, as I told all of my boys, exactly where I drew the line. I said that I would tolerate all kinds of mischief and stand by them, but once they stole they were on their own because as far as I was concerned stealing was terrible; the worst offence that they could commit.

It was a warning the lads took to heart because they have all turned out as honest as the day is long. Which is just as well in Jack's case. He was enough of a handful as it was.

From the moment he could walk Jack was full of devilment. One day, shortly after Bobby was born, and I was still in bed recovering, my cousin Nancy Fear looked out of my living-room window and shouted in surprise. A funeral procession was making its way slowly along the street outside, with mourners walking respectfully behind the coffin and led by a Salvation Army band. But then they were joined by two strangers. One was a drunk who had staggered out of a club as the procession passed it and the other was Jack. There he was in the thick of the mourners, toddling along with as much dignity as could be mustered by a two-year-old without any trousers.

'I'm not going down there to get him and show myself up,' Nancy declared, but she did – eventually.

For all his devilment Jack was still a likeable lad. People made a big fuss of him and he took terrible advantage of them. People like Mr and Mrs Curtis, who lived further down our street. They made a lot of Jack, but that still didn't stop him from taking a cauliflower from their back garden then walking to the front door and trying to sell it to Mrs Curtis.

As a youngster Jack was only really happy when he was out of doors. He spent hours bird-nesting, ratting or just walking through fields on the edge of town picking mushrooms.

At times I used to think 'God give me strength', but it was just

Jack's way; he was a born wanderer. Even when he was very young he sometimes went missing for hours. When he finally did come back he often couldn't tell us where he had been. But years later when we got a car and went for outings, he could tell us where every local road led, because he had already walked the lot.

One day, when Jack was just four years old a bus driver stopped my father and said 'Tanner, I've just seen your Jack at Guide Post.' Guide Post is four miles from Ashington and Jack had just taken it into his head to wander over there. Given Jack's love of country life and his dad's fondness for poaching, it is understandable that in later life he became a fishing and shooting enthusiast. Years later Jack's liking for those sports brought him into conflict with an animal rights group. Members of the group said he was a marked man and sprinkled broken glass onto a football pitch where Newcastle United were about to play, soon after Jack took over as team manager.

I know that Jack has his own point of view on the subject of guns and shooting and it is a point of view I have never argued with, except for once – the day he shot a young girl.

He was still a schoolboy at the time and I didn't even know he had a gun. I was so angry and shocked after the girl was hit, that I ordered him to get rid of it. He promised that he would, but much later, I learned that he had only hidden it away from me.

Because Jack's dad went shooting we were used to having guns around the house. So Jack was brought up to respect them and handle any gun with caution. But in spite of Bob's strict instructions Jack took his air rifle to school one day and fired it towards a nearby church. Unluckily for him, and the lass, Bernadette Reed, one of one of the slugs hit a fence and ricochetted. The wayward pellet hit her in the face grazing her eye.

Fortunately young Bernadette escaped with nothing worse than a nasty bruise, but the thought of how close she had come to losing her eye, because of Jack, horrified me. It was a terrible time. Jack was hauled before Mr. Hemmingway, his headmaster at Hirst Park Boys School, to explain why he had brought a gun to school. After he reprimanded Jack, Mr. Hemmingway suggested that I should go down and see Bernadette's father. I agreed and marched Jack down to the girl's home to apologise. When Bernadette's father answered my knock at his door, I told him who I was and said: 'This is the lad who shot your daughter.'

He looked at Jack for a moment and said 'So you're interested in guns son?'

Jack sheepishly answered 'Yes'.

'So am I.' said Mr Reed. 'Come on in and I'll let you see my guns if you like.'

It doesn't happen very often, but I was speechless!

CHAPTER SEVEN

Soon after my thyroid operation we moved house. I found the stairs in our Laburnum Terrace flat difficult to manage, so we swapped homes with a family living at 46 Hawthorn Road just a few streets away.

That move took me back to the same street where my mother had begun raising her young family thirty years earlier. Not far away was Hirst Park, a large thickly-grassed field hardly recognisable now as the same barren ash tip where I scampered as a tot and where my own young sons were now able to play. While we were living in Hawthorn Road I became friendly with May Hill, one of my new neighbours.

One day May called in and gave me an invitation which I just couldn't resist, even though it did scare the wits out of me. She asked me to go down one of the town's pits with her.

As a miner's daughter and as a miner's wife I was well used to hearing the men in my life talking about pit work. But, for decades past, women had not been allowed to work in mines. We weren't even welcome underground as visitors. Superstition had it that in pits, just as on board ships, a woman would somehow bring bad luck. So May's offer was a chance which would probably not come my way again.

She had been invited to look around Woodhorn Pit, in Ashington, by her husband Bob, who was an overman there. I agreed to go with her with a feeling of excitement and fear, because although I was going to see something few women had the chance to see, I was also aware that Woodhorn pit was the scene of Ashington's worst ever mining disaster.

Thirteen men lost their lives when an underground explosion shook the pit on the 13th of August 1916. On that Black Monday, eight deputies, and five miners died in the darkness of Woodhorn in an accident which was a shattering blow for a close-knit community like ours.

I thought that I knew all about Woodhorn and pit life, but when I finally went down for myself, I found it an eye-opening experience and one I have never wanted to repeat. The pit was probably no worse than any other, yet it was still terrible – dirty, dark and mouse-infested. I still hated mice.

After dropping 800 feet to the shaft bottom in a steel lift called a cage, we stepped out into what seemed to be a gale. I knew pits had to be ventilated, but I was taken aback to discover the force of that air. I also learned something else that day, something which I had suspected for a long time – that such a place was fit for neither man nor beast.

Afterwards, when I got back home I told Bob 'I don't care how small a pay you bring home. After seeing what you have to go through to get it I won't complain.' From that moment on neither would I have a word said against pitmen, they deserve all they earn and more just for going down that awful place.

My visit was made when the pit was privately owned by the Ashington Coal Company, a company set up in 1867 by William Milburn (no relation as far as I know, but I did say we were a big clan in Northumberland) and Jonathon Priestman.

I am told that after Vesting Day in 1947, conditions in the mines did improve, but I still never want to go back down to find out. It was horrible down Woodhorn and I was scared stiff, but even in my short time underground there were some light moments.

As we walked for what seemed like miles down the uneven galleries with our safety lamps glimmering in the eerie gloom, I could hear a soft, regular, footfall somewhere in the darkness behind.

Never coming closer, never fading away, it stopped when we stopped and started again when we started. It was like an echo, but it was not an echo of any sound made by us. Which ever way we turned it was always there, just beyond the range of our carbide 'glennie' lamps, but always moving as we moved.

I was scared and in those moments I came to understand the full effect of some of the pit ghost stories which older miners are fond of telling impressionable young apprentices down there in the bowels of the earth. One of the favourites in pits up and down the land is of the miner who becomes separated from his marras (workmates). As he tries to catch up to them he passes the entrance to an old gallery and looks down it. In the distance he sees the faint figure of a man. Thinking that it is one of his pals, he hurries down the gallery to meet him, relieved that at least he is no longer alone in the silent darkness.

He shouts a greeting to the figure ahead, but gets none in reply and when he gets close enough to see the figure clearly, he realises that it is a man wearing old fashioned clothes and carrying equipment which is no longer used in pits. Still without speaking, the figure looks at the miner, smiles and vanishes. At the same time the miner's glennie goes out...

Another is of a pitman coming away from the coalface and being passed by a grimy, stooping pitman on his way in. The miner on his way outbye can't make out the other's face but still offers a word of greeting. A brief nod is all he gets in return.

As the miner continues on his way out, he meets a deputy and asks who has just been sent to the coalface. The deputy answers that no-one, to his knowledge, has been sent inbye, so together they retrace the stooped miner's steps all the way along the roadway. There are no other exits and they pass no one on the way. Yet when they reach the coalface it is deserted.

As the story goes, the whites of each man's eyes glint in the sweep of their cap-lamps as they turn to look at each other briefly. Then stumbling and bumping, they charge back along the gallery to get as far away as possible as fast as possible...

Then there are the voices in the dark – sometimes low and murmuring, sometimes high and skittish like a woman's voice, sometimes like a child crying or laughing. Of course they are just rocks settling and timber props creaking. But in that confined, dark and dank, place it doesn't take an a lot of imagination to conjure up all kinds of wild things just beyond the flickering reach of a carbide cap-lamp's light.

Many a tough miner has set himself shaking by letting his imagination wander and I was beginning to get jittery myself about the mysterious sound following us. But our grinning guide took pity and put my mind at ease, explaining that our 'ghost' was only a pit pony which had latched onto us. Like every other pony in the pit it automatically trotted after the nearest light.

Ponies in the pit had been bred for the work on one of the Ashington Coal Company's farms and in many ways were better cared for than a lot of ponies on the surface. They were well fed and their stables were warm and dry. The ponies spent all their working lives underground, but contrary to what many animal lovers were fond of claiming, the ponies were not blinded by their lifetime of darkness. In fact they were kept in well-lit underground stables when they were not working and their eyesight was no worse affected than that of pitmen who returned to daylight at the end of their shift. The ponies, usually called Gallowa's whatever their breed, were regarded as 'four-legged miners' and treated very much as working partners by the pitmen who used them. Most miners had their favourites among the ponies and would bring them regular treats. For their part, most of the ponies had gentle natures and responded well to the kindnesses they were shown.

As we walked through the mine, I soon discovered why my Bob and other pitmen had scabs running down their backs, one for each bony bump of their spine. We wore pit helmets to protect us from overhead timbers and roofing, in Woodhorn's low galleries, but our heads still cracked on them again and again. Walking bent forwards with heads lifted up to shine our cap lamps on the roof soon gave us a crick in our necks. But we learned that it was a mistake to walk with our heads bowed forward to relieve the ache. For then it was our unprotected backs which made contact with the roof. That was how Bob came by those scrapes and scabs which I had to regularly clean out and bathe for him.

Eventually we reached the coalface and crouching down to peer through a lattice of wooden pit props I could see a miner, stripped to the waist, working a machine. Nearby a tin hung from a nail in a girder. In it was his bait, (mid-shift meal) probably a jam sandwich to be washed down with cold tea or water from a tin bottle. The box had to be made of tin and hung above the ground to keep it safe from scavenging mice and the occasional rat which shared the pit with the miners; just one more worry to gnaw at the men of Woodhorn.

As I watched one miner in a cramped, dirty, workspace, I could see that he was doing the same job as my Bob did at neighbouring Linton Colliery. Bob had talked many times about his job and I was as familiar with pit equipment and jargon as any miner, so trying to sound as matter-of-fact as I could, I called to the miner, who was moving a piece of equipment with his feet: 'Is that a J.B. or an Anderson Boyd?'

He burst out laughing and said 'What do ye knaa aboot it?'

I told him: 'I'm sick of hearing about them from my man.'

At the end of the tour we returned to the surface, grimy and blinking at the strength of the daylight. We gladly accepted an invitation to go to the colliery canteen for a cup of tea and some supper. We were choking to get rid of the taste of coal dust from our mouths.

When we asked where the canteen was our guide said 'Through that door there, hinny.'

Of course when we went through the door it didn't lead to the canteen at all. It was the pit baths full of naked miners!

But then that's just pitmen's humour for you; rough, but good-hearted.

And in those days a good laugh was something we needed desperately, for once again the country was at war. My three oldest brothers had joined the army and my other brother, Stan, was still working in the mines and playing football part time. His job was a reserved occupation so he couldn't join up. My husband Bob was in the same position and it rankled with him to be turned down when he tried to join the navy.

On the Saturday before Christmas 1943 I was out walking with Mother. She told me that she had sent off Christmas parcels to my brothers. Although she had no idea where her sons had been posted or when they would get the parcels, she was just relieved that they were at least on their way. She knew that they would be as welcome as the parcel which she had sent my father, Tanner, a generation and another war earlier, when he was a prisoner in

Germany; a parcel which he always said saved his life.

The next day Mother's tired, overworked heart gave out and she died – at the age of fifty.

CHAPTER EIGHT

After Mother died we moved back to Laburnum Terrace where Tanner still lived with Stan and my sister Gladys. Once again, as I had been doing from the age of ten, I became Mother's stand-in, but this time with no chance of ever handing the job back to her again.

Not long afterwards I became pregnant for the third time and when our new son arrived in 1944, we called him Gordon. We lived-in with Father until just after the end of World War Two when he got married again. By that time Bobby's natural skill with a ball was becoming obvious, especially to someone like Father. More than once in those days he told me 'Yer ganna be prood of that lad, Cissie.'

Father died before Bobby had gone very far in his football career, but he never had any doubts that Bobby would be one of the game's great names. He knew that the Warhorse inheritance had once again been successfully passed down to a new generation!

In Bobby's early years Father was a big influence on him. Bobby idolised Tanner and the two of them would talk for hours on end about football. They also had a special game which they played on Saturday nights. Young Bobby had to study the sports pages of that night's football paper and afterwards Father would quiz him throroughly about what he had read. Until the day he died, Tanner never lost his interest in the game. Towards the end of his life it became Bobby's regular Saturday night job to buy a football paper and then read the results to Tanner. Before Tanner died, he did a lot to encourage Bobby to improve his fitness and natural talent. He knew that speed would be as important to the young lad as his ability to control the ball and took him to sprint races to see the professional runners who Tanner was still training for the Powderhall Handicap. Bobby's treat at those races was to be given an 80-yard start by some of the top local sprinters of the day and try to beat them over the winning line.

Bobby also had four other heroes even closer to home – his four footballing uncles, Jack, George, Jim and Stan who, by the time Bobby was six, were all full-time professionals playing for leading league clubs. They thrilled Bobby with tales of how they had outplayed some of the top players of their day. Then they would take their star-struck nephew out into the back street and give him a kick-by-kick action replay of their latest matches.

Because Bobby had a natural talent which was obvious to anyone and because he was prepared to listen to good advice when he was given it, he was popular with older lads and men who enjoyed the game. One of them was Hammy Irwin. Hammy often played Sunday morning matches at the Hirst Park field which, a generation earlier, had been the spoil-ground where I had romped with my brothers. Many's the time that young Bobby stood on the sideline watching these games and aching to be part of them.

The players were grown men and teams rarely had eleven to a side. Usually, there were twenty, or more, to a team. It depended entirely on however many turned up. At times these games could also get pretty rough. Most of the players were miners; hard men used to very physical play.

I had mixed feelings when I heard Hammy shout, 'Come on lad', and bring Bobby into the game. I was pleased for Bobby's sake, but the sight of that little lad ploughing fearlessly into the thick of all those kicking and shoving men just made me worry all the more for his safety. For my benefit Hammy usually added, 'Don't worry Cis, I'll look after him.' He was as good as his word and Bobby never did come to any harm. But I still worried.

I know that in later life Bobby never forgot Hammy's kindness and for his part, Hammy was pleased to have helped Bobby at the start of what turned out to be such a successful career in football.

Bobby made less of an impression on his big brother Jack, who complained loudly and bitterly when I made him take Bobby with him when he went wandering in the country. At the age of eleven Jack considered that Bobby, two years younger than him, was thoroughly spoiled and a pain in the backside. He wanted to be off on his own, stretching those long legs of his through the woods and fields around Ashington, and not nursemaiding someone who he regarded as the family's fair-haired favourite. 'Aah'm not tekkin' wor kid. He's ower soft,' he complained. Jack just wanted to be away fishing, or looking for rabbits. For his part, although Bobby wanted to go with Jack, he wasn't as keen on the poacher's arts which Jack and their dad enjoyed so much. That made it even harder for me to force Jack to take Bobby with him.

'He'll just cry to come home before we've got anywhere,' Jack complained.

If I still insisted and made Jack take Bobby with him, he often gave Bobby a swift clout before they had gone very far and that usually sent him running home in tears, while Jack went on his own sweet way by himself.

Bobby's flair for football became really obvious when he was about nine and no-one was happier than me to see it developing. Football had been an escape route from pit work for so many members of my family and I wanted Bobby to at least have the same chance. As a result, whenever he wanted to see a particular game or get something connected with football, I usually made an extra effort to see that he got what he wanted. Jack saw that special attention as 'spoiling' his younger brother. Yet there was never any real envy between the two. They were such opposites that neither of them wanted what the other had anyway. I worried at first about Bobby's quiet ways. But in time I came to understand that he wasn't shy or reticent, just very self-contained.

While we were living with Tanner in Laburnum Terrace, Bob and me were offered our first colliery house in Chestnut Street. It was there that our fourth son, Tommy, was born in 1946. After three boys I had been aching to have a girl. When Tommy arrived, the nurse said, 'It's a lovely little boy'. If she had expected something gushing and maternal from me, she was disappointed. I answered huffily: 'It can't be lovely if it's another boy, and made up my mind there and then that enough was enough. I wasn't going to try for a girl any more! Actually, the nurse was right. Tommy *was* lovely – even if he wasn't a girl.

I have said earlier in my story that my father, Tanner, was a hard man – and so he was. But after his death something happened to make me see him in a different light.

My cousin Florrie Cobbledick found a diary in Tanner's house at Laburnum Terrace. My stepmother had died just a few months after Tanner, and a young lad, who was related to her, was scribbling in the diary. Florrie gave him sixpence for it and rescued it.

The diary was dated 1919 and in it Father had written down some of the experiences he went through during his two years as a prisoner of war – experiences he had always refused to talk about when he was alive. Florrie showed me the diary some time later and how strange it was to discover a new side to my own father from those buried memories. He had scrawled them in pencil over the yellowing pages of that old diary, which had been given to freed POWs by the International Committee of North American YMCAs. Tanner must have written it on his way home from the prison camp. Perhaps he had been ordered to commit his story to paper for some future pension or compensation claim, while they were still fresh in his mind, but whatever the original reason, they made me see him in a new way.

I don't believe that anyone could go through the experiences which he describes without being changed by them. So maybe I had been judging him too harshly for all those years. Yes, he was a hard man, but how many hundreds who were not as hard, had he seen die because of it, I wondered? And how does a father teach his sons and daughters such important lessons? Maybe one way is to be so tough that they must learn to fight for whatever they want out of life.

Tanner himself was certainly strong and stubborn. Even so, he still reached the depths of despair from which the prospect of death seemed better than the starvation, physical abuse and misery he went through in the POW camp. More than once his wish was very nearly granted.

The following extracts from his diary tell in his own words about what he went through and I think it is important to print them here to balance the view which I had of him when I was younger.

Private Tanner Milburn was captured during an early battle on the Somme – a battle which, by all accounts, went disastrously wrong. Four columns of British soldiers, each column three battalions deep, swept round the heavily defended German garrison in La Boiselle. The plan had been to obliterate La Boiselle with a huge mine. Then, as the main body of troops charged towards German trenches north of the village, a few bombing parties would be sent into the garrison to mop up any survivors.

The mine contained such a large amount of explosive that British commanders were ordered to keep their men well clear of the village as they charged towards the German trenches. But the attack plan failed and a terrible price was paid for the mistake; eighty per cent of the men either died or suffered wounds.

For some reason the mine went off in No Man's Land and the well-armed German defenders of La Boiselle were unharmed. The exposed Tommies were easy targets for the nests of German machine gunners in the garrison. All four commanding officers were killed and of eighty officers less than ten survived the day. Of all ranks, 940 men died and 1,600 were wounded. Not one officer or sergeant came out of the encounter uninjured.

The machine gunners in La Boiselle continued to strafe the ranks of fallen soldiers lying on the battlefield at the slightest sign of movement and only about 300 men survived that day without some form of injury.

By a miracle and a misdirected British artillery shell, Tanner Milburn was one of them. It was as he sprinted over the battleground past the Germans' number three line, that the British shell fell short of its target and showered him with earth – so much of it rained down on him that he was actually trapped by the weight of it.

Although he was stuck there, he was unhurt and also hidden from the view of the machine gunners.

Six hours later five Germans found him and dug him out. As they stood over my Father with bayonets drawn, the soldiers squabbled over whether to bother taking him prisoner or just kill him where he lay.

In the diary Father takes up the story:

I thought my time had come because one of them wanted to put the bayonet through me, but the others would not have it. Many a time in the years that followed I wish they had done me in. I was taken from that line to a dug-out further behind. In the dug-out were some Germans about to stand to. Just as they got out, the English started a bombardment and the German officer in charge had to drive them out with his revolver.

Some of the German soldiers were fainting, others were crying. So you can see what sort of soldiers they are and what sort of officers they have. The officer didn't say very much to me. He could speak broken English and he asked me what regiment I was in, but that was all.

I stayed in that dug-out all night, every minute expecting the British Tommies to come over. But they never came.

On the second of July I was taken to a chateau where a lot of British soldiers were lying on stretchers. They were wounded and crying for help where no help would come. I could have cried as well to see those poor fellows dying there when they might have been saved if they had been in our own men's hands.

I saw one poor officer in there with about ten wounds. He had only one shirt sleeve on. The rest had been torn away from him, I think by shrapnel.

He died as I sat beside him. I asked him his name, but he died with it on his lips.

I saw lots of English wounded there, but never saw a single doctor attending to them and I'll tell you why. It was because everybody had the wind-up that the English artillery was going to send some more stuff over.

On going out of the chateau we met a German officer who pointed a revolver at my head. He said 'You are the swines'. I stared straight at him and he rushed at me. He cut the numerals off my coat, pulled a ring off my finger and took my jacknife. I was not the least afraid and he let us go after that.

We got to the end of the communication trench on the Bafume (Baphume) road where an officer came up on a horse to speak to me just as I were coming out of the trench with a sentry. But the officer never spoke to me yet. Just as he dismounted from his horse over came one of our shells and carried him and his horse into an open field. It was a horrible sight.

When I came on to the Bafume road I had another close thing.

Some Germans rushed at us and they made a football of me. After that I was taken to a dressing station, where there were English and German wounded, for the night.

I met some more English prisoners here. One of them was very young - about 18 years old, I would say. He was not injured then, but he soon was. We were passing another dressing station when some Germans rushed at us with sticks and stones and lumps of dirt. We never spoke to them and the sentry was inside the dressing station at the time doing something.

One mad-brained German picked up a stone and let fly. He hit this kid square in the back.

I picked the kid up and the square head German just stood and laughed.

We marched away from there and came to a little village. I don't know its name, but the people were willing to give us butter, eggs and cigarettes, which the sentries would not let us have. But I did manage to get a bit.......

....Hunger, as they say, is a sharp thorn and I experienced it every morning. After 14 days we were taken to Dulmen camp. When we arrived there we got our first wash with soap and our clothes cleaned. We lay on the boards the first night then we went into the camp the next day.

We were isolated for seven days and we were inoculated five times. After seven days we were all in a very bad state from the lice and the lack of food.

At Dulmen we had three meals a day: two slices of bread, soup, barley water and coffee, tea or soup again at six o' clock. I never tasted such horrible stuff in my life, but what could a man do? You must eat it or die. Hunger is definitely a sharp thorn and one who has been a prisoner under the Huns knows it.....

....One day I was looking through the barbed wire when I saw Private J. Million, an old mate of mine with the 20th Northumberland Fusiliers battalion. He was the best friend I met in Germany. He brought me some baccy and some bread every morning for a week. But then we got orders to leave this camp. I was sorry because I would have been all right there until my packets came. But we left on the 14th day of August 1916 to go to a punishment camp. That camp was Heuberg in Baden. It was hell for English prisoners.

This is where I first met a swine of a field officer called Gotch. Nice man - I hope he is kicking up the daisies now.

In Heuberg we got a loaf of bread ten inches long and five inches wide to serve five men. It was not enough for one. The soup we got was made of cress and barley. Sometimes we got potatoes which seemed to have been planted before the Flood.

Once I saw one man get his soup and he pulled a mouse out of it. I nearly fetched all mine back again.

On the 27th August I was taken very ill. I saw the doctor but he said I must work.

Every morning for three mornings I went in and saw him. On the first of September I was in a dying condition. I could hardly stand up. We lined up for the doctor and this swine field officer Gotch came to inspect us before we saw the doctor. He said that the English prisoners looked all right. He came to me and asked what was the matter with me.

I told him and he called me a liar and a swine or pig and spat in my face. He told us that if the doctor signed our papers for work we would all be under arrest for seven days.

The doctor took my temperature, I think it was 38 and something in German. Anyway, I was sent to hospital and there I lay for three weeks.

The doctor said it was Darnkitter, (sic) or something. But in fact it was nothing other than a poisoned stomach from the food we had been given.

In that three weeks I had a very bad time of it and if it had not been for a mate of mine doing a little bit for me, I should have pegged out...

Father went on to work at a farm in Germany for the rest of his time there and he said he was treated fairly by the people running it. Even so, after his release at the end of the war he had to spend some time in hospital because of the damage done to his stomach by the foul food he, and the others, had been forced to eat to survive.

Nevertheless, he was among the lucky ones. At least he came home.

CHAPTER NINE

We lived in Chestnut Street for two years, but with my four lads all growing hard we needed somewhere bigger. That somewhere bigger turned out to be another colliery house in nearby Beatrice Street; 114 Beatrice Street to be exact. We lived there for the eighteen years which followed – and what years they were!

In those eighteen years that modest colliery house became a centre of public attention during events which delighted and shocked the football world.

Bob worked hard and provided for us, but there were six mouths to feed in the family and we never had money to spare. They were the days of 'make do and mend', when a good imagination was worth more than money.

I remember once, when the boys wanted some paint brushes I got a pair of scissors from a drawer and grabbed each of them in turn. Before they could stop me I had snipped a hank of hair from each of them which I fastened to a clothes peg. They made perfectly fine paint brushes as well as a lesson in economical living.

Of course there were times when the boys felt they were hard done by. One day they demanded to know why some lads living further down our street had been given bikes by their parents. They were no better off than us yet their parents could buy bikes, I was told very forcibly.

I had to admit that I was stumped. I couldn't give them an acceptable answer because I couldn't work it out either. The mystery was solved a few weeks later when a debt collector came and took the bikes off the other boys because their mother hadn't been able to afford them in the first place. That was another good lesson for my lads.

Looking back now on our home in Beatrice Street I can hardly believe how primitive it was. It had no bathroom at all, just a

A few tips on ball control in our Beatrice Street back yard for Gordon and Tommy as big brother Bobby looks on.

walk-in pantry with a cold water tap. Apart from the pantry, which we called a scullery, there was just one room downstairs, our combined living-room-kitchen. Yet those days in Beatrice Street were some of our best. It was a happy house and we were a happy family. In fact, at times we were positively hilarious, usually due to that husband of mine.

Bob had an allotment and took a special pride in being a good provider for his family. But sometimes he went too far for his own good. He once decided that we were going to have a Christmas dinner with a chicken as big as a turkey.

He got a white Leghorn cockerel and began to feed it up – and what a feeding that bird got! It was almost better looked after than we were. He was always taking it treats from my kitchen table and the more he fed it the bigger it grew. Eventually that chicken stood two and a half feet tall and was in absolutely prime condition. Of course the healthier a cockerel feels, the more aggressive it gets and being stuck in that hut all day only made its temper worse.

Eventually, Bob could only feed it by pushing food through the chicken-wire mesh of the cree while the ungrateful bird tried to make a meal of Bob's fingers. Its fresh water had to be poured through the wire into its dish with a watering can for the same reason.

Word about the size and evil nature of Bob's bird spread through the allotments and it gained quite a reputation among the other allotment men. So much so that when the day came for the cockerel to be killed Bob couldn't find anyone prepared to do the job.

He went all around the allotments trying to persuade men who usually did the slaughtering for allotment-holders, but couldn't find one willing to tackle our bird. If we were to have a chicken for Christmas there was only one thing for it – Bob would have to do the job himself. The method usually used on the allotments was to pull a bird's neck, so Bob rolled up his sleeves, took a deep breath and told our youngest son, Tommy, to open the cree door when he gave the word. On cue Tommy yanked the door back and Bob plunged in.....

Thirty years later Tommy still can't tell what happened next without gales of laughter. The sight of Bob and the cockerel squaring up to each other then launching into a no-holds-barred wrestling match, was like a scene from a slapstick film. Skin and feathers flew as the two of them rolled around the cree battling for the upper hand (or claw). The fight went on for several minutes before Bob was forced to retreat and the cockerel glared after him, daring him to come back.

Bob was panting and red-faced, as much with humiliation as effort, glowering at the cockerel which had just thrown him out of the hutch. Its beady eye had the glint of a long awaited victory in it – but not for long.

Bob couldn't take that sort of defeat lying down, especially in front of his youngest son. We did eventually get that bird for dinner – after he had turned to Tommy and ordered 'Haddaway home and fetch me gun, son.'

Bob was the most naturally funny man I have ever known, yet he never seemed to be aware of it. Whenever he walked into a room it only took moments for the laughter to start. Yet Bob often couldn't see what people found funny in the stories he was telling them.

Once we were having pigeon pie and under the hot crust was one of Bob's pigeons which had been a useless flier. He looked long and soulfully at the pie on the table in front of him and after much deep thought he leaned forward and confidentally scolded the steaming dishful – 'Aah towld yer te fly faster hinny'!

It was Bob's turn to fly though, on another occasion when he returned home after finishing a night-shift at the pit. Our youngest son, Tommy was going through the pet rabbit phase at the time. He pestered Bob to let him have one, but Bob wouldn't hear tell of it. Not that it made any difference. Tommy still went out and got himself a pair of huge Belgian Hares.

The black-and-white monsters were kept without Bob's knowledge in the coal shed next to our outdoor privvy at the bottom of the yard. Tommy knew that sooner or later his Dad was bound to find out. He just hoped it would be later, and that Bob would be in a good mood at the time. He was unlucky on both counts.

Bob discovered Tommy's deception in the early hours of a dark morning very soon after the hares had been installed.

He had just returned from work and headed straight for the backyard toilet. It had no light inside, but none was needed, he knew exactly where the paper lay. What he didn't know was that one of the hares had escaped from the adjoining coalhouse.

As he reached out in the darkness his hand closed on something large, warm, furry and wriggling. His bull-roar was enough to wake the street and in his surprise he didn't even open the privvy door – he burst it off its hinges as he charged out, stumbling as he ran; torn between the need to haul his trousers up from around his ankles and his desperation to get as far as he could from whatever creature it was that lurked in the dark corner of the smallest room.

Later, when he recovered his composure he reckoned that he had jumped six feet off that seat. Needless to say, the hares did not lodge with us for much longer after that.

Then one day Bob bought a pig. He was going to fatten it up and when it was slaughtered we would have more pork and bacon than we could handle, he announced. So he thought!

These were the 1950s and Britain was still suffering from post war shortages, so the prospect of all that pork had our mouths watering for ages as it grew fatter. Rationing was still in force, however, and before we could slaughter the pig we had to give up our bacon allowance.

Bob had a pal who would slaughter the pig for him and cut it up for a price. The agreement they reached was that Bob's pal would take his payment in meat and as he worked he kept cutting lumps off and throwing them into his bucket. He had a stutter and kept saying 'Th-that's n-n-nee g-g-good t-t-te y-yee.' By the time he was finished, his pile of meat was bigger than ours and I began to suspect that this was not quite the deal Bob had had in mind.

There are no secrets in pits, so Bob's workmates all knew when the pig was being slaughtered. As a result they badgered Bob for a morsel of his treat and every day before going to work he told me to put up an extra bacon sandwich for this mate and that mate. By the time everyone had taken their cut, we ended up with less meat than we would have had under our normal ration allowance.

Even the pit ponies knew Bob was a soft touch. He always took them a treat when he went down the pit – jam and bread or something like it. I knew he was fond of the ponies, but he still took me by surprise when he came into the house one day and announced, 'I've bought a horse.'

He not only had a horse, he'd bought a flatcart to go with it. I thought, 'Good God! You never know what he's going to come in with next.'

Even so, I have to admit that we did have a lot of fun with that horse and cart. On sunny days all six of us would pile on to the flatcart and go for a picnic. We were only three miles from the beautiful Northumberland coast, so we usually set out for the seaside villages of Newbiggin or Cresswell, singing all the way and hauling a big rubber sheet over ourselves if the weather changed and it rained.

We thought it was great, but Bob came in for some skit about that horse from his pals especially when one of them who did

Holidays, like this one to a Butlins camp, were rare. So when they came along I made the most of them. Gordon and Tommy are with me in the boat.

know a bit about horses looked at its teeth and announced that it was at least twenty four years old.

After that his mates used to say 'You shouldn't be on that flatcart, Bob. The horse should be up there and you should be pulling it.' In spite of their sarcasm, we still had a lot of fun with our horse Bobbie.

Although Bob was a good looking bloke I had always thought that with his pitwork and his hobbies, my husband would be too busy to bother with other women. But a time came when I began to have my doubts. Every Saturday night he went to one of the local clubs for a drink while I stayed at home with the lads. But when he came back from the club, after closing time at ten p.m., he didn't stay in as I expected. He went back out again and stayed away, sometimes into the early hours.

I said nothing about this strange behaviour. But it preyed on my mind until I became convinced that he was seeing another woman. I still said nothing, and after stewing about it for a while I decided that I would confront my two-timing husband and his fancy piece.

The next Saturday night he followed the same routine of the previous weekend. After he came back from the club and went out again, I slipped on a coat and followed. I tracked him down streets, across roads and along avenues through the sleeping town, until we reached his allotment. And there I met my rival.

It was Bobbie – that blasted horse of his!

Still unaware that I was there, he threw an arm around her neck and crooned into her twitching ear.

'Never mind hinny,' I heard him say. 'I'll not send you to the knacker's yard. I'll look after you to the end of your days. You'll not go to the glue factory.'

And as he nuzzled into her scratty neck I thought, 'My God! Isn't this great? Other men have mistresses and "fancy pieces" on the side, but my rival is a flaming horse – and an old nag at that!'

CHAPTER TEN

When his uncles and Hammy Irwin were not around to help and encourage him, Bobby practised on his own. For hours on end he kicked a small sponge rubber ball, or tennis ball against walls or down streets. Kick, trap, control, shoot. Shoot at walls, shoot at doors, shoot at a brick in the wall, shoot at a mark on the brick; left-footed, right-footed; hour after hour, day after day, week after week, getting better and better.

Even when I sent him on a message to the corner shop Bobby would first fish the ball from his pocket, drop it at his feet and dribble it all the way to the shop and back again.

So when, at the age of ten, he was picked to play for his school team, Hirst North juniors, it was hardly a surprise, but I was still delighted for him and even more so when he became team captain. Not long afterwards, Bobby also passed his eleven-plus exam, to win a grammar school place. But his joy at passing the grading exam turned sour when he was told which grammar school he would be going to – King Edward V1 School in the nearby town of Morpeth.

It was an old school with a fine reputation for its academic standards. Unfortunately King Edward V1 was a rugby school . No soccer was played there at all.

Bobby was absolutely shattered, for most of the eleven previous years he had lived and breathed football. Now he was facing the prospect of spending the next six crucial years at a school which didn't want to know about it.

Fortunately Mr Hamilton, the headmaster of Hirst North School, stepped in with a solution. He knew that Bobby had a special talent for football and that it would be a tragic waste of that talent if Bobby went to Morpeth. With Mr Hamilton's support I wrote to Northumberland education authority explaining Bobby's special needs and ability and he was given a place at

D. Armstrong.   A. Lavelle.   S. Urwin.   J. Straughan.   M. Cummings.   H. Dodd.   A. Smith.
R. Charlton.   D. Morris.   K. Millican.   R. Anderson.   D. Wrightson.   G. Crate.

Bedlington Grammar School, where soccer was on the curriculum.

It helped a little, but Bobby still didn't find his niche. At the Bedlington school, success as a sportsman was regarded as very much secondary to academic achievement. Unfortunately for Bobby, his mind was on football all the time and the conflict of interests meant that those days at Bedlington Grammar were not very happy ones. As it turned out, it was Mr Hemmingway, headmaster at Jack's school in Ashington, who arranged Bobby's first chance to break into big time soccer.

Jack was attending the Hirst Park Secondary School, which was only a few yards from our home in Beatrice Street. I was in its Parent/Teachers Association at the time and got on well with Mr Hemmingway. I had told him about the lack of encouragement Bobby was getting at Bedlington and Mr Hemmingway took the matter into his own hands He was an old friend of Manchester

United scout, Joe Armstrong, and advised him to come up to Northumberland and take a good look at this young lad called Bobby Charlton, who was playing for East Northumberland Boys at the time.

Joe came up and watched a game between East Northumberland and Hebburn and Jarrow. It was played on a terrible February day with ice covering the pitch at Hebburn School. But Joe said that he could see from Bobby's first kick of the ball that he had something special.

He was particularly impressed with the way Bobby controlled the ball and distributed it with his left as well as his right foot. It was a very mature skill for someone as young as Bobby, he said. Joe very soon came to the conclusion that his time had not been wasted by his old friend, Mr Hemmingway.

I was also at that game, cheering on the lads as usual, when, soon after kick off, Joe came over to me. He said that he liked what he had seen and asked if Bobby fancied going to Manchester when he finished school. Funnily enough Bobby might well have said 'no', but for one thing. Right up until that chilly day, Bobby's ambition had been to play for Sunderland. He was a great admirer of Len Shackleton's team and would have jumped at a chance to join it.

Sunderland also had a scout at that game between East Northumberland and Jarrow and Hebburn. But as it happened, the scout ignored Bobby and invited East Northumberland's goalkeeper, a young lad called Ronnie Routledge, to sign for them instead. Years later Ronnie, now secretary of Ashington FC, played a crucial role in bringing Bobby back to football after he said that he would never play again. But on that bitterly cold February day Bobby was really hurt to have been overlooked by Sunderland. Later, when Sunderland joined a long queue of major clubs trying to recruit Bobby, he had his own back. This time it was Bobby who did the turning down.

Nothing formal was signed after that first approach from Joe Armstrong, but Bobby did tell Joe that he was interested in joining United and the idea stuck. Yet, it was Jack, unpredictable as ever, who was the first of my sons to become a professional footballer. He had been training for a pit job for six months and in his free time played football for Ashington YMCA. I was watching him play in one game against a works team and would have been the sole spectator that bitterly cold day but for a man who was also looking on. After the game the man introduced himself to me and said that he was a scout for Leeds United. He asked whether Jack would be interested in going for a trial with Leeds. I didn't believe him at first. 'Wor Jackie?' I asked in surprise. I was amazed because although Jack enjoyed his game of football, he just wasn't the same calibre of player as Bobby. Jack was a good enough player to win a place on East Northumberland Boys team, but he hadn't made it onto the county side. I was pleased that he had been invited to go to Leeds United because my brothers were still living in Leeds and one of them, Jimmy, still played for the club. I knew that in Leeds Jack would be well looked after. Jack had just completed his time as a trainee fitter and was due to go underground to begin his apprenticeship the Monday after his game with Ashington YMCA, but instead, he went to Leeds.

The club liked what it saw and he was immediately signed up for Leeds by Major Frank Buckley. Jack came home for his clothes, went back again and that was it. He joined the club at the age of fifteen, continuing my family's long association with Leeds, and stayed there until the end of his playing career in 1973.

Bobby's big chance came in 1953. In that year he made his first appearance for England Schoolboys playing against the Welsh Schoolboy's side at Cardiff. He scored twice. The major football clubs were suddenly very interested in this newest talent from the Milburn clan. No less than 18 clubs wanted to sign Bobby including Wolves and Arsenal. At one point our Beatrice Street home was virtually beseiged by football scouts. The Arsenal scout, in particular, was always on the doorstep and Charlie Ferguson from Sunderland seemed to be behind me every time I turned round in my tiny kitchen. Charlie even got on to the Manchester bound train with us when Bobby was going down to sign formally for United. He hoped he might persuade us to change our minds at the last minute. But Sunderland had blown

Bobby at 15 played for England
Schoolboys at Wembley.

its chance back on that icy pitch in Hebburn when it went for Ron
Routledge instead of our Bobby.

He joined Manchester United for £10, the maximum signing-
on fee, although he could have had a lot more if he'd been
interested in just the money.

The high-pressure tactics employed by some of the more
unscrupulous scouts included some pretty lucrative bribes. The
biggest backhander offered was £800. In 1953, the year of the
FA's ninetieth anniversary, that was a fantastic amount of money,
especially to a family like ours which had never had much money.
But we wouldn't accept the bribes. It may seem naive and
unworldly now. I suppose it did even then, because everyone

knew it went on. Many clubs got around the fixed wage agreement by stuffing a fistful of cash into a players back pocket. Yet the plain fact of the matter was that taking bribes was illegal and we just couldn't bring ourselves to do it, even if they were accepted as a fact of professional football life in those days. We were honest, working-class people with a very clear idea of right and wrong and no amount of money was going to change that.

Originally I had wanted Bobby to go to Arsenal because the club had an excellent youth policy and youngsters of fifteen and sixteen, like Bobby, were very well looked after. Bobby, too, was attracted by the glamour of the London club, but Manchester United also had a sound youth policy. Matt Busby had introduced a policy of recruiting schoolboys and putting them through a proper 'apprenticeship' with the club. It was a new idea; until then, works teams and minor league sides had been the more usual source of players.

So, after we had discussed all the pros and cons, on 16th June 1953, aged just fifteen, Bobby signed amateur forms with Manchester United, beginning a playing career with the club which lasted almost twenty years.

News of the signing did not endear Bobby to Mr James, his headmaster at Bedlington Grammar School. He wrote to me saying that he thought it was a mistake for Bobby to throw away four years of study.

Although I knew Bobby had made the right decision, I also recognised that the headmaster had a point. Football is a risky business and it made sense for Bobby to have a few GCEs to his credit, if possible.

The compromise we eventually reached was that Bobby would continue with his studies, but at Stretford Grammar School in Manchester and with everyone happy with that arrangement Bobby began to settle into his first days as a (although the phrase had not been coined at that time) Busby Babe.

After almost two years in Manchester, Bobby reached the age of seventeen and was invited to sign on as a professional with United. In those early days of his apprenticeship with Manchester, Bobby played first for the club's 'A' and 'B' teams against works sides, then went into the Central League playing for Manchester United Reserves.

It was about then that my outspoken ways got me into trouble again - and this time with Matt (now Sir Matt) Busby. I have always thought, and still do think, that Matt Busby is a really nice man and I couldn't see us ever crossing swords. But it seemed to me that Bobby was as good as the other Busby Babes and yet time and time again he was overlooked when the selection was made for the first team.

Other players who were the same age as Bobby and had the same amount of experience were making it to the first team, but not Bobby and I got a strange idea into my head. If there was no difference in their ability or experience then it had to be some other reason and the only difference I could come up with was that Bobby was the only non-Catholic among them.

I'm not the type to dwell on my thoughts, so I grabbed the bull by the horns. I went to Matt and asked him straight: 'Is Bobby being left out of the team because he isn't Catholic?' I couldn't have been more blunt! Neither could Matt. I knew from the expression on his face that I had put my foot right in it – once again. I could see that I had really offended him. 'How could you even think something like that?' he stormed. 'You are an intelligent woman, Cis. Don't ever ask me anything like that again.' He was right and I was wrong, I know that now.

Good as Bobby was, he was competing against some of the best young players of the day for his place in the first team. Matt knew far better than me when Bobby would be ready to make that move and I would have to keep my opinions to myself until he was ready.

Matt decided that Bobby was ready for his first team debut in October 1956. In that game, ironically against Charlton Athletic, Bobby scored twice. It was a fine start to a long career – but still just a start. All that Bobby had learned from his grandfather Tanner, his uncles and everyone else who had encouraged him in Ashington, was just preliminary groundwork. The real business of learning his craft was just beginning.

In the expert hands of Jimmy Murphy and Bert Whalley,

assistants to Matt Busby, Bobby was put through a make-or-break programme of training and coaching. In the end Bobby's determination won out and it was make, not break. Bobby took the advice given to him and benefitted from it.

On the other hand his brother, Jack, still stubborn, argumentative and rebellious, found it harder to settle and find his best form. He clashed with coaches and managers at Leeds time and time again. Raich Carter, Bill Lambton and Jack Taylor had all been in charge at Elland Road and, in their turn, each had tried to get through to that rebellious son of mine. Eventually it was two years National Service in the Guards which taught him the real meaning and value of discipline. But it wasn't until Don Revie took over as Leeds' manager in 1963 that Jack really found how to use discipline to improve his game.

Blunt-speaking Don took the wind out of Jack's sails, shortly after taking over, by using an unexpected tactic – he praised him.

When Don had played for Leeds alongside Jack, during the club's bleak 1961-62 season, Leeds almost went down to the Third Division and Don had been scathing in his criticism of Jack's lack of commitment and discipline. He said Jack didn't deserve a place on the team and wouldn't have one if he was manager. So a couple of years later, when Don did move into the manager's seat, flattery was the last thing Jack expected after being summoned into Revie's office. Yet that was what he got.

Revie told Jack that he had in him the potential to play at international level, even to be as good as his brother Bobby. Only his bloody-minded attitude stood in the way. Don's words struck home and almost overnight Jack's game began to get better. As Leeds United's fortunes improved, Jack's reputation grew until, as Don had predicted, England's selectors began to think seriously of recruiting him.

Gangling and gritty, his reputation for hard, physical football contrasted totally with Bobby's image of skill and sportsmanship. Yet the selectors did eventually decide that both had just what was needed by what became the most famous of England's national soccer sides.

Bobby's first international was a major event and I was invited to go down to it with Bob - at Manchester United's expense.

Bob's sister Kitty was living with us at the time after their mother had died and she was able to babysit Gordon and Tommy for us. Bob was not all that interested in the game, but we had never stayed in an hotel before and it wasn't going to cost us anything so he agreed to go.

We went to Manchester first and were met by Joe Armstrong who told us we had been booked into the Queen's Hotel. Dinner was over by the time we arrived at the hotel, but we were shown to a table which had been laid out specially for us.

Bob stared at the table, wide-eyed. He looked down at the ranks of sparkling knives, forks and spoons and in that deep droll voice of his said: 'What's all this artillery for?' I said to him: 'Just start out over and work your way in'. But of course, the inevitable happened.

Joe and I began to talk about football and became engrossed in our conversation. Bob was left to his own devices and, of course, by the end of the meal with just the final course to tackle, Bob had run out of the right kind of 'artillery' and ended up attacking his ice-cream with a knife and fork.

He drowned his embarassment with a few drinks. They cheered him up, but rather too much. As we left the dining room he got his eyes on some women in evening gowns who were heading for the hotel ballroom. Bob decided that he was in the mood for dancing into the early hours.

I soon put a stop to that and dragged him off to our room where he made two fresh discoveries.

The first was that we had twin beds. It was Bob's first encounter with twin beds and he soon came to the conclusion that they were just not natural. He heaved the two single beds together, certain that this was how they should have been in the first place.

The second discovery was made when he looked under the dressing table.

'That's not what you think it is either,' I told him. 'It's a pink wastepaper basket and don't you dare use it for anything else.' But he seemed unconvinced and I lay wide awake for what seemed to be all night long in our doubled-up twin beds, just waiting to grab him if he dared to do anything which would show me up.

Eventually I did doze off, then I heard Bob's voice. 'Cis, Cis. There's somebody trying to get into the room,' he whispered.

'It'll just be the maid with our tea,' I answered.

Just before we had gone up to our room I had told Bob to order an early morning cup of tea for both of us. The thoughts of a pretty young maid in attendance at his bedside quite caught Bob's imagination and he willingly agreed. Realising then who it was at the door, he sat up straight, smoothed the crumples from his brand-new pyjamas and said: 'Come in'.

He was genuinely expecting a dolly bird and I could hardly keep my face straight when the maid came in. She was about sixty, wore a mop cap and had a face like thunder.

'Did you order two teas?' she demanded. Bob, disappointed and cowed, meekly answered 'Yes'. 'Well you gave the wrong room number,' she said icily. 'I have just delivered two cups of early morning tea to a spinster's bedroom – she threw me out!'

Bob didn't have much better luck with the steward on the train which took us to Cardiff later that day. He loved tea and at home drank gallons of the stuff. The steward was bringing little cardboard cups of tea to passengers on the train. But before we were half-way to Cardiff our table was hidden beneath a mountain of them. The steward got so fed up that he finally left and returned with a tea urn which he dumped on the table in front of Bob.

A little further along on the journey we were passing through the Rhondda Valley and I remarked on how red the soil was there. Completely straight-faced, Bob informed me: 'Yes. This is where they grow red cabbage.' I was so green I believed him!

Bobby's next game for England Schoolboys was against the Republic of Ireland side and was played in Portsmouth. We went down for that game too and after the match I asked Joe Armstrong about Bobby's chances of being selected again. There were three more games to be played and Bobby's place on the team was not a certainty.

Joe said that he was happy with Bobby's dribbling and he had no doubts about his shooting power – in the game against Wales Bobby had knocked out the young Welsh 'keeper with one of his goal shots. But Joe felt that Bobby's slowness on the turn was a serious weakness which needed to be put right before he could go much further.

When we got back to Ashington I tried to get some of the local runners there to give Bobby some extra training to speed him up. When I couldn't get anyone to take on the job I decided to do it myself. I knew well enough what had to be done, I had seen Tanner training sprinters often enough in the past!

I went with Bobby to Hirst Park, just across the road at the bottom of Beatrice Street and paced out 80 yards. Then I got Bobby to run that 80 yards, turn and run back, then 60 yards and turn, then 30 yards and turn. Gradually his speed on the turn increased.

I suppose that to a stranger it may have looked odd to see a fifteen-year-old lad training like that with his mother, especially in those days, but this was Ashington and everyone there knew I was football mad. For years I had been kicking footballs around parks and back streets in that town, usually with my skirt tucked into my knickers and with a bunch of lads, so there wasn't as much as a raised eyebrow among the folk there at the sight of me and Bobby in the park.

A few years later I tried to encourage Bobby's brother Gordon in the same way. Gordon too needed to be quickened up and I took him and our dog Chuck into the park every morning before school.

Chuck would bark with excitement as he ran around the park with us and eventually it became too much for one man whose home overlooked the park. He stopped me one morning and said: 'Look Cis, we don't mind *you* running around here – but not that bloody dog!' Chuck stayed at home after that.

During the 1950s Bobby and Jack both came in for growing attention from the press and public, which could have made my other sons, Tommy and Gordon, jealous. But just the opposite happened. Gordon, in particular, hero-worshipped his big brothers when he was a schoolboy. Even to the point of doing some crazy things just to win their praise. One day he took his life in his hands and jumped from a high harbour wall at Craster on the North Northumberland coast, straight into the icy North Sea, when Jack jokingly dared him to do it.

On another occasion he had gone with his brothers into the country to shoot rabbits. They shot one on an opencast coal site, but it was raining heavily and a muddy ditch lay between them and the kill. What they needed was a retriever, and poor, eager-to-please, Gordon was cruelly nominated for the job by the others.

Gordon hero-worshipped his big brothers when he was just a schoolboy.

He eagerly scrambled over the perimeter fence and waded through the muddy ditch and squelched onto the sticky quagmire beyond. The laughing brothers back in the car urged him on through the mire.

'Quick, quick, there's somebody coming,' they yelled. Of course, there was no one: they were just trying to scare him to add to his discomfort and their entertainment. But in his panic, as Gordon struggled to get back, he dropped the rabbit into the ditch and watched, horrified, as it slipped below the surface to vanish out of sight beneath the filthy water.

He's the fatso on the right i the back row!

Mortified at this loss of face Gordon shouted, 'What should I do?' His brothers by now were helpless with laughter. 'Dive for it', came the instant reply. And without argument or hesitation, Gordon plunged into the dirty dike and fished out what by then was a very bedraggled bunny. He returned to the car dripping wet, clutching the tatty catch, to be greeted by hoots from within. But Gordon didn't mind – it was all good 'clean' fun as far as he was concerned.

So much happened in those 'Happy Days' of the 1950s; the war was over and Britain was on the road to recovery, rationing had ended, Bobby and Jack were beginning to make their names as professional footballers, there was an air of optimism across the land and the future seemed bright for all of us.

Then, in 1957, I discovered that I had cancer.

CHAPTER ELEVEN

I was 45, I had cancer of the breast and I believed that I was going to die. In those days cancer was a subject mentioned only in hushed tones, if at all. Ignorance of this terrible disease fed my fear of it and I gave in to a black anguish when the worst was confirmed.

That miserable time for me began while I was washing blankets at home. As I worked I became aware of a lump in my breast. I prayed that my worst fears would be unfounded; that it would turn out to be a benign growth; that I could go on looking after my family, that I would live to see all of my sons grown up and so much more that I seemed to be on the verge of losing.

After consulting my family doctor I was sent to hospital to have the lump removed and analysed. Later I returned to the hospital to have my stitches taken out and to be told the results of the tests. All my life I have always believed in, and practised, plain speaking, but this was the one time I needed soft words. Unfortunately the hospital doctor was even more blunt than I am. In fact, 'blunt' is too kind a word. He was nothing less than brutal.

As a nurse prepared to carefully snip the stitches from the wound, the doctor casually told her, 'I wouldn't bother, that breast's got to come off anyway.' I couldn't believe what he was saying, or that he hadn't even attempted to break the news to me gently.

My cousin Nancy Fear had come to the hospital with me to lend moral support, and how I needed her now!

We left the hospital, but I couldn't face going home to Bob and the lads just then, so we began to walk the streets of Ashington. We walked for hours together, crying all the time.

Only when I thought all my tears had been cried out could I go home and tell my family. I'd never held anything back from the lads, but they were still young and I did my best to break the bad news more tactfully than the doctor. I told them, 'Now you've all got to be good boys because your Mam's got to go into hospital again.' I never have been a good liar and the lads knew straight away that something was very wrong.

Gordon, who was only about thirteen at the time, looked up and said: 'Are you going to die, Mam?' I couldn't hide my own fear and I started to cry all over again.

A mastectomy operation was my only hope so I went to Ashington General Hospital and the breast was removed. It was a major job and for a while I was very ill. But as I progressed along the road to recovery I became more and more confident that the doctors had caught the cancer in time. I knew in my heart that I *was* going to make it. I was not ready to part company with this world yet, not by a long chalk, I told myself. There was too much still ahead for me, I felt so sure of it.

Fifteen of us had gone to that hospital for the same treatment, but as I lay there looking around the ward I just knew that whatever fate had in store for them, I was going to be all right and I was not wrong!

When I was discharged from the hospital, I was still quite weak, but the boys did their best for me. They also helped me come to terms with my changed physical condition in their own inimitable fashion.

Jack was so sympathetic! He stopped calling me Mother and started calling me 'lefty'. The falsie that I was given to wear to restore my shape to usual also gave rise to more mirth. Once, Jack took the family washing to a launderette and sat there among the women watching my falsie going round and round in the washing machine porthole. We laughed and laughed about it when he got back home and told me about it. I had to laugh. It was either that or cry.

After the operation I wasn't able to be as active as I had been before, but my limitations were not severe enough to spoil things for me completely. I was eventually able to go dancing again and that meant a lot to me. It also gave me another good laugh.

It was a real hoot to see the expressions on some of the men's faces as they found themselves bouncing off me when we came

A rare occasion when the footballers in the family, and Bob and I, were all together. This was for a 'World of Sport' broadcast. From left to right – Jimmy Milburn & Stan Milburn in the back row. George Milburn, Jack Milburn, Wor Jackie Milburn, Bob and me, Jack and Bobby.

together on the dance floor. They must have wondered what on earth I was made of. I could have told them: birdseed.

At least that's what it seemed like: just a bag of birdseed.

Yes, the 1950s were certainly a time for tears and for laughter, a lot of it taking place in that little Beatrice Street colliery house of ours. Primitive it may have been, but what it lacked in facilities it made up for in a happy atmosphere. It was also 'Liberty Hall'.

When I woke in the mornings I always had to ask how many there were for breakfast, because I never knew for sure. The lads liked to go to dances with their mates and if any of them missed their bus they were always brought back to our house and put up for the night.

Once. after Bobby had played a match in Scotland, he travelled back in a bus with some of his team-mates. Unfortunately for them the bus' fanbelt broke on the way home stranding them for most of the night.

I had been at the same game, but I travelled by car. It was morning before the bus could be fixed and by then its passengers were ravenously hungry and tired. Ashington wasn't too far away, and 'Liberty Hall' beckonned.

Just before eight a.m. they descended on the Beatrice Street. As fast as I could make them, my egg-and-bacon sandwiches were being wolfed down and people were collapsing into exhausted sleep wherever they could find a bed, chair or floor space.

As well as players, there were some reporters who had travelled with them, including Tony Stratton-Smith, a quite brilliant sports feature writer with the *Daily Sketch* newspaper. I apologised to him for his less than grand accommodation, but he was charming about it. 'I've never had so much fun in my life,' he told me and after that day we became firm friends.

That is why Beatrice Street was great. Everyone was welcome and no-one, no matter how grand or how modest their background, felt out of place. They seemed to be instantly at ease when they walked through the door.

That certainly applied to one little lad who came into my home in 1953.

It was Coronation year and the folk of Beatrice Street, like people in towns and cities all over the land, decided to hold their own street party. Ours was a bit different though.

Before Coronation Day, Bobby had been invited to referee a match at a Doctor Barnardo's orphanage in Cullercoats, a few miles from Ashington, on the Northumberland coast.

Children at the orphanage were obviously well looked after, but I felt that it was such a shame that these children were missing out on the kind of family life that we were enjoying. After the match there was a sing-song at night. A priest played the piano and that was the only time I have ever heard 'Abide with me' played in swing-time.

We all had a great night, but after having met these kids we wanted to do something more for them. So, when we got back home we told our neighbours in Beatrice Street about the orphans.

The upshot was that they were all invited to the Beatrice Street Coronation Day party. Our idea was that for at least that one special day, each of the orphans would have a family and a home to go to.

We collected three pence a head for weeks and organised money-raising events to pay for their transport out to Ashington and a few treats for them when they got there.

The temporary member of the Charlton family was a coloured boy of about ten, called Michael. Our plans for an outdoor street party had to be scrapped, like so many others on June 2nd, when it poured with rain, but we had made arrangements in case that happened and held the party in Hirst Park school hall instead.

But when it was time for the party to start, little Michael didn't want to leave my house. When I asked why, he told me: 'I just want to stay here.'

The school hall, crowded with other children, shouting, playing, eating, arguing, was no novelty to him. That was something he experienced every day in the home.

What he wanted was the feel of real family life in an ordinary house. He hung back for as long as he could before reluctantly going with us to the party – I could have cried; he was so hungry for what we took for granted: an ordinary home and an ordinary family.

Afterwards many of the folks in Beatrice Street kept in touch with the youngsters from the orphanage. Some years later it closed down, but the friendships made on that Coronation Day continued for a long time.

Michael stayed in contact with us until he grew up he moved to Kent and we lost touch with him.

Yes, Beatrice Street in the fifties was a friendly pit row and never friendlier than on New Year's Eve when almost everyone went first-footing.

Bobby and Jack made it a rule to always try to be home in time to celebrate the arrival of a new year together and they kept up the tradition until they married. They usually timed their journeys so that they could meet at a railway station and travel home together. On the eve of 1958 Bobby also arrived with two of his team-mates, David Pegg and Eddie Colman. He had just spent Christmas in Doncaster with David and his parents and was returning the hospitality he had enjoyed.

In those days New Year was welcomed at Ashington with as much gusto as food, drink and sheer physical stamina could sustain. On New Year's Eve and on into the early hours of New Year's Day, every door in the street was open to first-footers. David and Eddie couldn't get over how even total strangers could just walk in to any household and be treated like long-lost sons.

After taking his pals to a few homes nearby, Bobby came in laughing and announced that David was kissing every girl he met, he was so excited by the atmosphere and the friendship which he had discovered.

The boys had such a great time that later they went up to the local co-op store and asked the counter assistant to recommend a gift they could buy for me.

I was given two little jugs and an ornate brass ash tray. The jugs have disintegrated over the years, but I still have the ash tray and I treasure it. I treasure it because two months after those happy lads presented it to me, they were dead and my own son was injured – all victims of the Munich air disaster.

CHAPTER TWELVE

On the sixth day of February 1958 a chartered B.E.A. Elizabethan aircraft struggled to clear the blizzard-swept runway at Munich Airport. It had earlier landed there to refuel on its way back to England from Belgrade. Passengers on board included the now-famous Busby Babes. The Babes had just beaten Red Star in the second leg of a European Cup game by a 5-4 aggregate and earned a place in the forthcoming semi-final. The scoreline in that second-leg match against Red Star had been 3-3. Two of Manchester's goals had been scored by Bobby and the third by Dennis Viollet.

The twin engines of the Elizabethan, code name ZULU UNI-FORM-609(G-ALZU), roared and it picked up speed on the slush-coated Munich runway, but suddenly the brakes were slammed on and the passengers inside were thrown forward. The aircraft slithered to a halt. A second attempt to get airborne was equally unsuccessful.

Over the on-board intercom, passengers were told in measured, even tones by co-pilot Captain Ken Rayment that a mechanical fault was going to delay their take-off. He invited them to disembark and wait in the airport lounge while the hitch was sorted out. A few minutes later they were recalled and a third attempt was made to get the Elizabethan off the ground. This time there was no return to earlier exchanges of cheerful banter between players, officials and pressmen on board - just a tense silence.

Once more the twin engines roared above the howl of the blizzard outside. With the release of its brakes the Elizabethan surged forward and rapidly picked up speed.

Take-off speed was reached and passed, yet the aircraft remained sluggishly indifferent as pilot, Captain James Thain struggled with the controls. The speed of the aircraft inexplicably

The Busby Babes just before the tragedy of Munich. David Pegg was acutely embarrassed about being presented with a bunch of flowers just before the kick-off.

The tangled wreckage of the B.E.A. Elizabethan aircraft after the crash at Munich which so nearly claimed Bobby's life. Harry Gregg, on the right, found Bobby wandering around and took him to hospital.

dropped from 117 knots to 105 knots and even the passengers realised that something had gone terribly wrong.

According to an inquiry held later, a build-up of ice on the aeroplane's wings was responsible for what happened next.

Still 'glued' to the ground the aircraft hit a perimeter fence at the end of the runway and ploughed into a house before disintegrating. Eight of Bobby's team-mates died from their injuries either in the initial crash or during the days that followed. So did eight leading sports writers, club officials and Captain Rayment.

Miraculously, some passengers were thrown clear as the spinning aircraft was torn apart. Among them was Bobby. He had been sitting next to Dennis Viollet near the front of the high wing Elizabethan. In the impact he was thrown clear as it disintegrated and landed a hundred yards from the wrecked aeroplane. He was still strapped to his seat and his only physical injury was a gashed head, but terrible emotional injury was to follow as the scale of the tragedy became clear.

Lying near Bobby in the snow was Jackie Blanchflower, Dennis Viollet and Matt Busby. Matt was much more seriously hurt than the others. But at least they were alive.

I always worried when the boys were flying, but on the morning of that tragic flight I was more worried than I had ever been in my life. I just couldn't settle, but neither could I explain why.

Something was happening which I couldn't put into words, a black worry had settled on me and I just couldn't shake it off. I waded through the thick blanket of snow in Beatrice Street to a neighbour's house on the opposite side of the back lane and did something I had never done before.

Although I was on friendly terms with my neighbours I never bothered them with my troubles. Yet this day I poured my heart out to one of them, Mrs Marshall. I told her that I was worried and how I wished Bobby was back home.

Not long after I returned to my house, Ted Cockburn who ran a newsagent's shop nearby, came into our yard. Ted had often travelled to London with me for international matches and was a good friend of the family. He was as white as a sheet and he didn't have to tell me why.

'It's Bobby isn't it?' I asked. He answered 'Yes, but I wanted you to know before it went on the placards. The *Evening Chronicle* (our local evening paper) has put out bills about Bobby being in a plane crash and I wanted to make sure you knew first before I put them up.' I told him that I hadn't been told of it, which was true, yet in my heart I had known all morning.

The first television and radio reports said that there had been no survivors. I didn't want to believe what I was being told and switched everything off to keep the news I was afraid to hear away from me.

I told Ted that I was going to telephone Manchester United for the true story and we went to a call box outside his shop. But the telephone lines had been brought down by heavy snowfalls and I couldn't get through.

As I stood there in that cold call-box an image which I had kept at bay until then, began to fill my mind. I could see Bobby lying in the snow, so cold and not moving. That awful picture took over and I couldn't see anything else. I became hysterical, I went berserk, crying and shouting for Bobby in that useless phone box.

Ted got me out and brought me home. Not long afterwards a policeman came to the door and said, 'Don't believe anything you hear. We will keep you posted. We will tell you exactly what is happening.' In the meantime, my other son Jack was in the dressing room at Leeds getting changed after a training session.

Arthur Crowther, Leeds' secretary at the time, came into the dressing room and said, 'The Manchester plane has been in a crash. They don't think there are any survivors.' Unbelievably Jack was refused leave to come home. So he grabbed his coat and marched out. He picked up Pat, his wife of one month, and together they caught the first train for Newcastle.

Still not knowing whether or not Bobby had survived they couldn't believe the callousness of other passengers in their carriage who were discussing the crash. Their main concern was how much compensation should be claimed from the airline for the loss of the famous Busby Babes.

When Jack and Pat arrived in Newcastle they headed for the

116

Haymarket bus station to catch a connection for Ashington.

At the Haymarket a newspaper vendor was selling a late edition of the *Evening Chronicle*. Fearing what he was going to read, Jack bought one and saw in the front page story that Bobby was among the survivors. People must have thought he was crazy, because right there in the bus station he grabbed Pat and together they danced a jig of joy.

I'd had no contact with Jack, but I knew he was on his way. As people tried to console me at home, I just kept saying, 'Jack'll come, Jack'll come.'

Not long afterwards Bob Turbill, one of our local policemen, came to the door waving a piece of paper. It was a note from Bobby relayed through the Foreign Office.

It read, 'Alive and well, see you later,' and was signed 'Bobby'. Then Jack walked in, grinning.

We still couldn't get any more news than that so I made up my mind to go to Manchester. My sister-in-law Kitty was still living with us at the time and she agreed to look after the family for me. Even so, it was not going to be easy. Heavy snowfalls had by then forced the cancellation of bus services and we had no car. But I had to get to Manchester, somehow, some way.

It was Ted Cockburn who found a way. He helped me to hitch a lift from a newspaper delivery van driver who brought the next day's papers to his shop just before seven a.m. It looked as if there wouldn't be any other form of transport out of town that day so I was grateful for the lift.

The delivery van went back to its main office, Kemsley House, in Newcastle, just a stone's throw from Central Station, where I caught the Manchester train. When I got to Manchester, club officials told me that Bobby just had a cut on his head.

An aircraft was chartered to take relatives of the victims out to Munich and I was offered a seat on it. But I wasn't able to go. My doctor had warned me to go only if Bobby was desperately ill. It was just three months after I'd had my cancer operation and he said I was nowhere near fit enough for the flight.

While other families were flown out to the Rechts der Isar Hospital, in Munich, I had to content myself with making a tape-recorded message for Bobby and sending it out with them. My recording in broadest Geordie dialect apparently gave more than just 'Wor Bobby' a good laugh.

I stayed on in Manchester to give what help I could while waiting for Bobby to be brought back. There was a lot of work to be done at Old Trafford.

At first I went into the office and helped to prepare tickets for the club's next fixture game. The match was against Sheffield Wednesday and when the programmes for it were printed they appeared with eleven blank spaces. The Football Association said Manchester United must field a team for the game and Jimmy Murphy, Matt Busby's able deputy, had to do his best to pick up the pieces that were left of the devastated dream which he and Matt Busby had worked so long and so hard to turn into reality.

Jimmy was broken-hearted, as were the rest of the staff, but when he visited the critically-injured Matt at Rechts der Isar hospital the boss had whispered to him, 'Keep the flag flying, Jimmy, until I get back', and keep the flag flying he did, in spite of his own deep grief.

As he tackled his unhappy job over the days that followed, Jimmy often said to me, 'Make us a cup of tea Cis,' and I knew what he meant. I put a little drop of tea in the cup and filled the rest with whisky. It helped him to keep going during that terrible time.

But it was a pitiful sight to see him wandering around the empty football ground at night, all alone with his thoughts in the darkness.

The bodies of those who died in the crash were brought back to Manchester and laid in the club's gym. I was given the job of showing their parents where the caskets were. I represented Bobby at the funerals of Eddie Colman and David Pegg, the two lads who had been so excited by their Geordie New Year only two months earlier.

They were horrible days. So many players, pressmen and officials all gone: Roger Byrne, Tommy Taylor, Tom Curry, Willie Satinoff, Mark Jones, Billy Whelan, Geoff Bent, coach Bert Whalley and trainer Walter Crickmer among them. So many

David Pegg's mother sent me this photo of her by the grave
not long after I'd been to his funeral.

friends all lost, so much talent wasted.

Eventually Bobby was well enough to return home. Jack
telephoned me and suggested that we go down to London together
to meet him. He was due to arrive at Liverpool Street station and
we were there waiting.

When Bobby got off the train he was a pathetic sight. He just
stood beside his case looking lost. The platform was cordoned off
but the station was swarming with pressmen and spectators. Jack
said, 'Let's just get him away from here.'

We gave the reporters and photographers the slip, first by
driving to my sister Gladys' home in Huntingdon, and then up to
Jack's house in Leeds.

The next day Bobby and me got on the train to Newcastle. In
our carriage was a sailor who talked and talked about the crash.
Bobby remained silent and withdrawn. Eventually the sailor

119

dozed off. When he saw that the sailor was asleep, Bobby turned to me and said, 'Look Mother, I am going to tell you about it now, but I don't want it ever mentioned again.'

He told me how he had been thrown out of the plane still strapped to his seat but he couldn't remember anything more until he woke up in the hospital. He had been told afterwards that Harry Gregg, the goalkeeper, found him wandering around covered in blood from the cut on his head. Since that day, Bobby has never mentioned the subject of Munich to me again.

Not all of the players were killed outright. One who had been brought from the wreckage badly injured, but alive, was Duncan Edwards. Duncan was quite simply the greatest footballer of his generation. He was twenty-one years old and in the previous five and a half years since being recruited by Matt Busby and Jimmy Murphy, he had become a footballing legend. Matt himself described Duncan as 'the complete footballer'. He became the youngest First Division professional when, still eighty days short of his sixteenth birthday, he played for Manchester United against Cardiff City in April 1953.

Duncan captained England Schoolboys and the Under-23s and played for England in a full international when he was just seventeen years and eight months old. There can be no doubt that he would eventually have captained England and gone on to further a career which seemed destined for heights of glory. Duncan was Bobby's hero and, more importantly, a good friend.

In Bobby's early days with Manchester United he was not making a lot of money, unlike Duncan who played regularly for the first team.

Duncan was such a considerate boy. He knew that Bobby's pride wouldn't allow him to accept charity, but he also wanted to help out his young friend. His solution was not very subtle, but it worked. If Duncan thought that Bobby needed a new shirt he simply bought one, supposedly for himself, and then said it was too small for him and gave it to Bobby.

Twenty days after the Munich crash Duncan died from the massive injuries he had suffered. Bobby was still at home in Ashington and when I read of Duncan's death I hid the morning

A BACK street, a handful of soccer-struck boys, and a famous footballer, back in his home town after 12 days in which his name has rarely been out of the headlines.

The town is Ashington, and the footballer Manchester United's Bobby Charlton, one of the few to escape from the Munich disaster without serious injury.

Yesterday Bobby was reunited with his parents in Beatrice Terrace—and one of his first questions was: "Mum, is there a football in the house?"

After a day or two he may take the ball into a local park, but meanwhile he is content to drop a few hints to those hero-worshipping boys in the back lane . . .

There were many letters waiting at home for Bobby including a Valentine. "It is from a girl down South. She has written before, but we've never met," he said.

At my persuasion, Bobby agreed to pose for newsmen who had been pestering us for a photograph shortly after his return from Munich. He never wanted to play another game of football again, in spite of what the story said.

121

newspaper before Bobby got up, then made his favourite breakfast of egg, bacon and mushrooms.

When Bobby came downstairs he said, 'Where's the newspaper?' I told him, 'Oh, it hasn't come yet, get your breakfast.'

I still couldn't tell lies convincingly, even white ones. Bobby looked me in the eyes and said, 'I don't want any breakfast. Duncan has died, hasn't he?'

'Yes', I answered, but there was no need. He already knew.

The press had begun to call at our house in Beatrice Street seeking interviews with Bobby. He didn't want to see any of them, but I said he would have to get it over with some time. I reminded Bobby that when he was younger he had wanted to be a sports reporter and in different circumstances it might have been him there asking for a story. He agreed reluctantly and went out to be photographed in the back lane with a football. A handful of youngsters in football strip were pictured with him as he obligingly tapped a leather-case football over to them.

The story which appeared the next day said that one of Bobby's first questions on coming home was 'Mum, is there a football in the house?' But when he came back indoors after the cameramen and reporters had left, Bobby announced that he was giving up football for good. He said that he had lost all of his mates and he never wanted to play football again.

Meanwhile at Old Trafford Jimmy Murphy was doing his best to rebuild Manchester United. He had bought Ernie Taylor from Blackpool as a first step, then Stan Crowther from Aston Villa. But he also needed every good player already on the club's books, even if it meant bringing on some young players much earlier than planned. That included Bobby and Jimmy began to step up the pressure for him to come back to Manchester. I got a telegram urging me to tell Bobby that if there was nothing wrong with him, he should be back in boots.

For as long as he could, Bobby made his head injury an excuse for not going back. He had stitches in the wound, but refused to go to the doctor's to have them removed.

Eventually I asked our family doctor, Dr McPherson, to call casually at the house and have a word with Bobby. When he did, he said, 'You know, Bobby, I was in the Air Force during the war and I saw many of my pals shot down and the only thing to do about it then was to go straight back up.

'Your name is in football and football is flying for you. My advice is go back to the game and start flying again. There is nothing wrong with you that time won't heal.'

Shortly after the doctor left, Ronnie Routledge called in to see Bobby. As I have already mentioned, it was Ronnie who, six years earlier, had caught the Sunderland scout's attention instead of Bobby, during that East Northumberland Boys game in Jarrow.

Ronnie had a football tucked under his arm when he arrived at our house and he said to Bobby, 'Fancy coming down to the park for a kickaround?'

They went off together and when Bobby came back later he simply announced 'I'll go back to Manchester.' But it was still a long time before he got over the Munich experience and a long

It took Bobby some time to get over the air crash.

time before he found the form expected of him.

Before Munich Bobby had played upfield ready to shoot at goal. In the re-formed team he was positioned inside forward, inside left and a number of other positions before he eventually settled down as a deep-lying centre forward. Three months after the disaster the new Manchester United had incredibly won through to the final of the FA Cup. David Pegg's parents went to Wembley to watch the game against Bolton Wanderers and before the kick-off Bobby told them, 'Every goal I score today is for David.' Unhappily he didn't manage to score a single goal and when he came off the field he was heartbroken. He told Mr and Mrs Pegg that he hadn't been able to keep his promise because every time he looked down at the ball to kick it, he saw the face of one of the boys killed at Munich.

In reaching those days I had also come to that time in life every parent faces when their children become adults and leave the nest to make their own way in the world.

Jack had married his girlfriend, Pat Kemp, a month before Munich and on Saturday the 22nd of June 1961, Bobby also became a husband. He married a Manchester girl, Norma Ball, at St Gabriel's Church, Middleton Junction.

So, two of my boys were now married men and both soon began families of their own. Jack and Pat, living in Leeds, were first. They gave Bob and me our first grandchild, John, on the 30th January 1959. Bobby and Norma's firstborn, Suzanne, arrived just after Guy Fawkes Day, the 6th of November in 1962. But that still left Gordon and Tommy at home, two lively lads to be looked after until they too were ready to leave, which meant plenty of work and worry yet for this mother.

Jack and girl-friend, Pat Kemp,
who later became his wife.

Bobby's wife, Norma, and their first child
Suzanne. (*Manchester Evening News*)

CHAPTER THIRTEEN

I put up with having whisky thrown over me, I endured the foul language and I managed to ignore all of the insults - except for one. Then, to my everlasting shame, my temper snapped and I whacked a big Scot across the face as hard as I could. And my reason? Well I'll come to that in a moment, but first let me set the scene.

I travelled as often as I could to international matches when Jack or Bobby were playing and because they were such big events I always liked to dress in my best for them. So, for a start, I was more than a little annoyed at having whisky flung over me by that drunken Scot during this particular match. The game itself was a bad-tempered affair, with England losing and Jack ending up in hospital with a badly-injured ankle.

I had been sitting with Jack's wife Pat and Mrs Ramsey, whose husband Alf (later Sir Alf) was managing the England side at that time. Mrs Ramsey left first to make her way to the dressing rooms and she was subjected to a lot of verbal abuse from some of the Scotland fans. Then Pat and I went down to try to find out whether Jack would be coming home or staying in hospital overnight. The fans, who had given Mrs Ramsey such a rough time, turned their attentions on us. Pat walked away from the crowd, but I stayed to find out what was happening about Jack. The insults continued for my benefit and I managed to ignore them until one of the jibes touched a raw nerve. I know it's irrational, but I have always been highly sensitive about my four sons' lack of hair. Their father was bald and I know that they probably inherited their thin thatches from him. But I have never quite been able to shake off the feeling that somehow the failure was mine; that I was responsible.

So, what was the insult, you ask? Well, one of the Scots called Bobby a four-letter name. But that didn't hit the nerve; what made me lash out was the five letter word he put in front of it. Bobby

Charlton was a 'BALDY ****', he shouted at me.

Unfortunately for us both he yelled it within striking distance and before either of us realised, my hand cracked across the side of his face. Thumping him was simply a reflex action which I regretted instantly, not just because I was immediately surrounded by that hostile and largely drunken crowd, but because I had let my instincts get the better of my beliefs. I have always held that there can never be any excuse for violence on the pitch or the terraces and I felt that I had really let myself down.

I was alone in the middle of that angry crowd and for a moment it looked as though things were going to get very ugly. A woman, who had been with the man whose face I slapped, shouted: 'You're no lady!'

My fins were up and I yelled back: 'If he's yours then you can't be a lady either.'

Luckily for me Billy Bremner's father-in-law was nearby and before any more could be said he came to my rescue. Billy had shared digs with Jack in their early days at Leeds and the two have stayed firm friends ever since. Billy's father-in-law ploughed through the crowd and hauled me out before anyone realised what was happening.

Afterwards I was so ashamed of what I had done, but it was only what any mother would do in those circumstances.

Before his playing career ended, Bobby was capped 106 times for England, a record beaten only by Bobby Moore, and then by just one cap. Jack's International career began later than his brother's. He got his first cap when he was twenty seven and went on to get 34 more.

The early 1960s saw the start of Bobby and Jack's greatest playing days. Yet the new decade began with both of them off form. Bobby had been capped for England in 1958 and selected for the 1958 World Cup Squad, under the managership of Walter Winterbottom, although he wasn't picked to play.

Part way through the 1959-60 season Bobby lost form and was dropped to Manchester United's Reserve team. He also lost his place on the England team. Bobby worked hard to find top form again and his efforts were rewarded with a return to the first team and a place in the 1960 International at Hampden. In 1962 he was selected for the World Cup in Chile, this time as a playing member of the squad.

England got through to the quarter final of the contest, but were knocked out by Brazil. At that time Leeds United were still struggling to get out of the Second Division. They succeeded in 1965.

In the 1964-5 season Jack also got his first cap for England. The game, against the old enemy, Scotland, ended in a 2-2 draw. But Jack turned in a performance which justified the selectors' confidence in him and proved that, although quite late in the day, he had emerged as a world-class centre-half.

That match was also special for another reason. It marked my debut as a Fleet Street columnist!

When the news broke that my two sons had been picked to play for England it sent the nation's newshounds wild. They seemed to never be away from my home in Beatrice Street, as they all tried to outscoop each other with new angles on the 'Charlton story'. Then someone at the *Daily Sketch* newspaper had the idea of signing me up to write a match report on the big game. It was an attractive idea and I took no persuading. Two days before the game I got onto the six forty-five p.m. London-bound train at Newcastle Central Station with my husband Bob and Anne Buchanan from the *Daily Sketch*. But I was not prepared for what happened when we arrived at Kings Cross station.

As Bob and I left the train I looked up the platform and saw a big crowd of cameramen.

'There must be somebody important on the train,' I told Bob. As we walked towards them I looked around, trying to see the personality they were waiting for. Suddenly camera flashguns began to flicker among the pack of photographers and reporters and as we got nearer to them it dawned on me that they were waiting there for us.

The *Sketch* wanted us to be kept well away from rival newspapers so once we had managed to get out of the railway station, we were taken straight to the Waldorf Hotel where a room had been booked for us. Such luxury! What would Mrs Fowler, my old

Bob and me on our way to the first game in which Bobby and Jack played together for England, a home international against Scotland in 1965.

employer in Watford, have thought of her 'guttersnipe' if she could have seen me then?

Still, old habits die hard and I couldn't help thinking of the poor soul who would have to clean the shoes which had been left outside the room opposite ours.

The next day, just before we left for Fleet Street to be shown around the *Daily Sketch* offices, I noticed that the shoes were still there, but polished to perfection.

Later, *Sketch* photographer Terry O'Neill was assigned to take pictures of Bob and me at Wembley. On the way, we stopped at the Old Bull and Bush pub and I sat next to a good-looking chap who seemed vaguely familiar. It took a few moments for it to click. It was Robert Beatty, the actor.

Back at the *Sketch* offices I saw our photographs being developed before returning to the Waldorf escorted by our 'minder' Don Smith. At the Waldorf it took all of 6ft 5in Don's bulk to fend off the pack of waiting reporters intent on spiking the *Sketch's* guns with their own Charlton story.

We took refuge in our room and had to stay there until the coast was once again clear. To keep them off our scent we were taken on a car tour of London seeing all the famous sights and, for the first time, seeing them as a tourist in comfort and ease rather than as a skivvy snatching a glimpse of a better life, for a few hours away from her chores.

The Houses of Parliament, the National Gallery, Battersea Park, we visited the lot, and we passed Quentin Hogg (now Viscount Hailsham) pedalling along on his three-wheeler bike.

We returned to the Waldorf for tea and fitted in an interview with the BBC before going to see the musical Camelot at Drury Lane. In spite of all the bustle and rush, however, I couldn't help noticing that those highly polished shoes were still exactly where I had seen them that morning. 'Strange?' I thought.

The next day, match day, I looked out of my room and sure enough the shoes were still there. I couldn't contain my curiosity any longer and stopped the first member of the hotel staff I could find. 'Those shoes haven't moved in two days and I'm a bit worried, do you think something might be wrong?' I asked. He smiled a knowing smile and said: 'No madam, nothing is wrong – that's the honeymoon suite!'

When we went downstairs we found the hotel was bursting with activity. It was filled with exotic-looking people. Wealthy Arabs seemed to be everywhere and a reception for a society wedding was in full swing, with the women guests parading a rich collection of beautiful dresses, fine furs and glamorous hats.

I bumped into another actor, Raymond Francis, who played a detective in the television series *No Hiding Place* which was topping the ratings at that time.

A lot of Scotland's supporters had also booked into the hotel intent on celebrating the weekend in style and no doubt expecting England to be thrashed by the boys from over the Border. So it was with delight that they recognised me wearing my new in navy blue and white dress. Oh, what a gaff. How could I have done it? I was so pre-occupied with choosing a nice dress for the occasion I had completely overlooked the fact that it was in Scotland's colours! How they laughed at my expense. Which is more than Jack did when he saw it. He gave me a right ticking off, but nothing he said dulled the thrill of that day for me.

Just before the kick-off, rain, which had been falling earlier in the day, eased off and the sun shone on Wembley. Then the teams emerged onto the field. It is hard to describe how it felt to see both Jack and Bobby out there together in England shirts.

Imagine a mother's pride. Add to it a patriot's passion and top that heady mixture with my Milburn's love of the game and you begin to approach what was going on inside me. Even though the match ended in a 2-2 draw, Bobby managed to score one of the goals and I was on cloud nine at the final whistle.

Champagne emotions gave way to the real stuff that night when the *Daily Sketch* held a dinner party at the Blue Angel Club for us and our friends. A band played and sang a calypso written specially for us. The celebrations went on until three in the morning, when we returned to the hotel tired, but happy. We were up again just a few hours later and I went with Bob for a walk along the Thames embankment, before heading for Fleet Street and the job I had come down to London to do.

In the editorial office of the *Daily Sketch* I began to write my report of the previous day's match. This is what appeared in the *Daily Sketch* the next day, 12 April 1965:-

No guest sports writer can ever have sat down to describe a game with such a red face as I have this morning. Because it's just impossible for me to describe Saturday's International at Wembley without naming my son, Bobby, as the man of the match.

That first great goal, his perfect pass to Jimmy Greaves for the second, and the unique experience of seeing him play so brilliantly in both attack and defence puts Bobby among the greats in my mind.

And if you call me big-headed I can only tell you that when I kissed my son after the game and told him how well he had played, he replied: 'I've waited 12 years to hear you say that Mam'.

But I wasn't only proud of my sons yesterday. (I'm sorry but I shall have a word to say about Jackie too, later). I was so proud to be English I thought I'd burst.

For sheer guts and fighting spirit I can never remember seeing a game like it, and if we hadn't lost two men we would have routed Scotland.

When poor Ray Wilson was carried off my concentration as a spectator was overcome by feelings as a mother.

Ray is Bobby's closest pal and I was sure that seeing him carried off in such obvious pain would throw anyone as loyal and sensitive as Bobby.

But after the injuries, Bobby, like all the other players, became more determined than ever.

I can't remember such a personally emotional day in a lifetime spent watching football.

In the morning I was all butterflies, unusual for me. But I worried myself sick about Jackie.

After all, it might have been his brother's 57th cap but it was Jackie's first and I passionately wanted him to show that Wembley lot what he was made of.

My worries eased within minutes of the kick off because Jackie seemed so cool and relaxed. And after 25 minutes my secret dream came true.

That wonderful telepathy which my boys have always had between each other since they were little lads went into action...and so did my new white hat, flying into the air as I shouted in that Charlton goal, scored by Bobby from Jackie's pass.

People say daft things at such moments, but when my husband, Bob, reminded me that the doctor said excitement was bad for my heart I said 'Oh, shut up.' All I knew was that Jackie had shown the world he knew what this game of football was all about, and I was glad his wife had made the decision not to tell him before the match that their little boy John, had had an accident which meant six stitches being put in his head.

Back to the match... I admit I called Gordon Banks a few Geordie names when he seemed to help that Denis Law goal over the line.

But I took them all back when he made so many brilliant saves after that. But that was nothing to the names Jackie called me after the game. 'How could you?' he said when he looked at me...and I realised that my new navy-and-white outfit was in Scotland's colours. Saturday was the kind of day every mother dreams of when she's skinning her knuckles getting the mud off her lad's shirt, or diddling the housekeeping for a new pair of football boots.

When the family and I celebrated over champagne in the Blue Angel night club, and every member of the Charlton family was mentioned in a wonderful calypso, I couldn't help saying to myself 'Cis, for a colliery family we have come a long way.'

It was a fascinating experience to write that story and the editor gallantly offered me a job after seeing the proof of my story and Terry O'Neill's photographs.

The next day we headed back to the North East and our kind of normality. But what a fabulous memory that weekend has been to treasure and recall over the years since.

My other sons, Gordon and Tommy, had by this time left school and were making their own way in life. Gordon had tried to follow his two elder brothers into professional football and for a time showed a lot of promise. He took the same route into the game as his uncles and brother Jack, by signing for Leeds United. But it was not to be and six months later Gordon left Leeds to return to Ashington.

Both Gordon and Tommy inherited their father's hankering for a career at sea. Gordon joined the Merchant Navy first and stayed in it for two years. Tommy followed and stuck at the job for a year, but just to prove that he could do it. After that year he'd had enough, the salt water was flushed out of his system and he happily went back to a career on dry land, first as a colliery fitter

Tommy and a favourite whippet.

and a few years later as a mines rescue brigadesman, then officer.

Maybe their dad would have been the same, but Bob was a miner and during the war years that was a reserved occupation. His dream of going to sea stayed just that, a dream, until it was too late for him.

Having been denied his crack at the wider world, Bob built his life around his own world of home and work. Bob loved his allotment and like all the gardeners I know, seemed convinced that the less he spent on it, the sweeter its produce tasted. It goes almost without saying that the shed he built on his allotment was constructed from scrap wood, held together with nails which had been prised from old timber and hammered straight. I never knew Bob to buy a piece of wood or a single nail all his life.

The shed was home to Bob's pigeons and what a home those birds had to come back to. They had every comfort Bob could offer them – as long as it didn't cost money. Not that he was mean, he was just part of a generation which had learned the hard way the truth of the old saying that a penny saved is a penny earned.

Bob's economies often raised wry smiles. One of them involved not using glass to repair a broken window in the pigeon cree. Many of the allotment men put paper up at their windows to keep out draughts, but only Bob's pigeons had a copy of the Mona Lisa smiling sweetly down at them. Jack later remarked on a television programme about our family that everything Bob ever made, big or small, was always put together with six-inch nails – and he wasn't exaggerating. Bob had by now begun to realise that he had a knack for making people laugh and when he was in the fettle he played up to it. But always in his own dry, straight-faced way. He had hundreds of invented stories about goings on in the pit which no-one could ever quite manage to separate from the truth. Fact and fantasy were both delivered absolutely deadpan by Bob – and the join never showed.

Once we were boarding a train when his face fell. 'Cis,' he said solemnly. 'Do you know what we have forgotten to pack? The Brylcreem.' His crumpled face remained fixed. A crumpled face topped by a totally bald pate!

He could play me like those blasted fish he was so fond of catching and I would still bite every time. And not just me. Bob was once travelling to Linton pit on a colliery steam train nicknamed 'The Linton Flyer'. It was the early hours of morning and although villagers sometimes hitched an illicit lift with the 'Flyer', this time the only people in the compartment were Bob and some apprentices.

Working at a pit is depressing enough without having to go down at that unearthly hour so Bob decided that the boys needed cheering up. Anyone else would have chatted to the lads about football, or girls, or cracked a joke to get them smiling. But Bob was too dry for that. Instead, he pretended to fall asleep. After a few minutes of gentle snoring he suddenly snorted. Pretending that he was still half asleep, he asked one apprentice 'Is this the day the Dandy's delivered?'

He kept his face straight as the apprentices struggled to find an appropriate reply after having 'accidentally' discovered Old Bob's secret – that he still took a children's comic.

Even men who had worked with Bob for years never quite

knew when he was kidding, no matter how far he allowed his imagination to roam. Once when I was shopping I bought a tin of pineapple chunks and one of Bob's mates, who happened to be in the shop, burst out laughing, but wouldn't tell me why. Later I learned that Bob had his workmates convinced that I had a passion for pineapple chunks. According to Bob I even took tins of them to bed where I sat with a can opener cutting the cans open and greedily spooning out the contents.

'I could put up with that,' he had indignantly told his mates. 'But what gets me is the way she just slings the empty tins under the bed. There's dozens of them there!'

In those days miners worked in teams and jointly negotiated with their bosses a price for digging a certain yardage of coal. The money they made was then shared out among the team. At sharing-out time the men often pocketed some of the money for themselves and gave their wives the balance. 'Keepie-backs' were common enough, but Bob had to turn even that old-established practice into one of his straight-faced jokes.

'Me and Wor Cis had a row last week', he declared. 'So I'm finin' hor half-a-croon.' He pocketed the money with a flourish and left the other men wondering, once again, whether Bob was being serious or whether he did have the nerve to fine his missus for nagging, and, no doubt, whether they dare do the same.

Although Bob had no real interest in football he took quite a liking to football shirts. Apart from being comfortable to wear for work they had an added appeal, they cost him nothing.

When Jack or Bobby came home he often asked for their old football shirts to use at work and at work his mates would say, 'Are you centre-forward or centre-half tonight Bob.'

He never wanted to play or even watch football, but I have a sneaking suspicion that in his poker-faced way he was grinning inside again when he wore those shirts; grinning at the irony of his outfit, grinning with pride and grinning with satisfaction – satisfaction that the original wearers of those shirts had earned them through very special talents, talents which had saved them from having to go down that terrible black hole in the ground as he had to every day of his working life.

A family celebration in the 1960s brought us all together in Leeds. In the front row with me are Gordon, Bobby and Jack, while their wives, Norma and Pat, flank Bob at the back.

CHAPTER FOURTEEN

Bob's indifference to football was a puzzle to many people, especially in those exciting days leading up to the 1966 World Cup contest when it seemed that the whole country had gone football crazy.

Even a little mongrel dog called Pickles became an international celebrity because of it.

While Pickles was out for his daily 'walkies' he began to rummage in a hedge, as dogs often do. But Pickles' owner noticed that he wasn't sniffing about the hedge for the usual reason. He could see that the dog had found something in the undergrowth and when he investigated, to his amazement, he pulled out the Jules Rimet World Cup trophy. The trophy had been stolen earlier and by unearthing it from the hedge where it had been dumped, nosey Pickles turned himself into a celebrity whose story and photograph were seen the World over.

Press interest in the competition was fierce and anyone who had even a remote connection with it was, inevitably, drawn into the publicity circus. That, naturally, included the whole Charlton family. Over the years, particularly since Munich, we had become used to reporters dropping in at Beatrice Street and we counted some among our old friends. But even they were surprised by Bob's attitude towards the one subject which the whole country was talking about.

It came to a head when England met Portugal in the World Cup semi-final. For while the rest of Britain went through ninety minutes of agony to find out whether England would make it to the final, Bob went down the pit to work instead.

BBC sports commentator, David Coleman, was so amazed that just before a recording of the match was broadcast, he telephoned Linton Colliery and asked Mr Murphy, the manager, if Bob could be brought out to see the game. Remember, these were the days before video recoders were available and it was Bob's only chance to see the game.

Mr Murphy, naturally the men always called him 'Spud', agreed and Bob was summoned from the coalface to the surface in the middle of his shift to watch Bobby and Jack in action on the nearest television set, which just happened to be in 'Spud's own house.

Afterwards, the press gave Bob a tremendous amount of praise for his 'dedication' to duty. Here was the kind of worker the country needed more of, they said. Which was a bit of a laugh really, because Bob didn't mind missing the match one little bit.

In spite of any discomfort Bob may have felt sitting there in the manager's front room, I was pleased that he did see England's semi-final against Portugal, because in that game he was seeing football at its best. I only wish that it had been the final. The game had everything in it that I loved about football. Eusebio was brilliant, so was Bobby. The Portuguese were skillful, but also looked so happy to be playing. I was there to support England, but I must admit that I had a real soft spot for Portugal's team, they had such lovely smiles and they were true sportsmen.

Before the game Eusebio said how much he admired Bobby's playing and during the match he showed that he meant it. Bobby scored both of England's goals in that game with shots that were classics of their kind. The first was driven in low and hard, the second travelled 25 yards before hitting the roof of the net.

The goals were impressive, but I was just as impressed to see that Eusebio was also clapping Bobby. What a tremendous gesture and what a tremendous sportsman.

Although they were two goals down I knew the game was far from decided. I knew those smiling Portuguese players would fight to the last second and there were plenty of thrills to come. With only minutes left before the final whistle my heart leaped into my mouth and, like so many times before, on and off the field, it was Jack who put it there. England's defenders came under tremendous pressure from the Portugal forwards and Jack gave away a penalty when he handled a header from Torres which was bound for the back of the England net. Eusebio took the penalty

My proudest day was when Bobby and Jack walked onto the
pitch in their England shirts.

and gave Gordon Banks no chance of stopping it.

The tension was terrific right up to the final whistle. But by the end of the match it was England who had won the appointment with West Germany in the final.

I was so excited for myself and for the boys, but I couldn't help regretting a little that there had to be a winner at all from two such deserving teams.

While the final against West Germany had a more dramatic climax, I agree with those experts who afterwards said that it lacked the attacking excitement of that semi-final, when both Bobby and Eusebio were given enough elbow room to produce some superb soccer. In the World Cup final Bobby and West Germany's Franz Beckenbauer, had been ordered to mark and contain one another. The result was that they simply cancelled each other out.

Bob had not been bothered whether or not he saw the semi-final, but I did manage to persuade him to go to the final at Wembley with me. I can't help wondering how many other people would have given their right arm for the same chance.

Even though I got Bob to come to the final I still didn't get all my own way. I had insisted that Bob must buy a new suit and a new trilby hat for the big occasion and gave him strict instructions to leave his beloved flat cap at home.

Well, I must give him this, he did actually go out and buy a new trilby. But somehow he managed to lose it just before the big game. 'Never mind, Cis,' he told me. 'It's lucky aah've put me owld cap in me pocket just in case.'

I watched all of England's qualifying games yet one of my fondest memories from that unforgettable contest is of the opening ceremony. Seventy-five thousand people were waiting, in brilliant sunshine, in the Wembley ground and the Queen, accompanied by Prince Philip and Sir Stanley Rouse, President of FIFA, the international football federation, officially opened the championships. Each of the sixteen competing countries was represented by schoolchildren dressed in the team colours, who marched and waved flags before gathering in the middle of the pitch to perform an absolutely perfect display.

The massed bands of the Brigade of Guards played and trumpeters from the Household Cavalry, sounded a fanfare. All this and World-class football too. What a time it was!

I had started out by travelling down from Newcastle for each of the World Cup games, but Jack convinced me that I should book into an hotel in London for the duration of the contest. He knew that it was going to be difficult to find an hotel room and told me that if I was beat for somewhere to stay I should contact a friend of his called Jack at the Great Northern Hotel.

I tried everywhere, but couldn't get a room, so eventually I went to the Great Northern and asked for Jack. I was still out of luck. The hotel receptionist told me that it was Jack's day off.

'Just my luck,' I thought and asked the girl if there was a room available. She was sorry but they didn't have one room left. I said, 'Alright,' and turned to leave. As I reached the door the girl asked, 'Who should I say called when Jack comes back?' I answered, 'Mrs Charlton, Jack Charlton's mother.'

It was as if I had said a magic password. The receptionist's manner changed completely. She said, 'Oh, would you like a room with a bath?' I was infuriated to think that as an ordinary customer I couldn't have the room, yet as Cis Charlton I could.

Like the tot in high dudgeon over the wrong starch, the scullery maid fuming over the 'guttersnipe' insult and the protective mother sideswiping the drunken Scot, my temper flared once again and also, as usual, it was soon regretted.

I snapped 'No you can keep it,' and stormed out. Unfortunately I had just thrown away my only chance of a room and I had to travel down from the North East for the rest of the World Cup games until the final.

Just before England met Portugal in that crucial semi-final, Jack telephoned and asked me to have tea with him before the match. The team had been stuck in the Hendon Hall Hotel since 8 July and he was aching to see a friendly face which didn't belong to the England party.

When I got there Alf Ramsey, England's manager, came over to me and announced that he had arranged transport to Wembley for me.

He also added: 'You're not going home tonight either, I have booked a room for you here.' I was really impressed to think that in spite of all the pressure he must have been under, Alf would take time out to think about me. But that is just the kind of man Alf Ramsey is.

Matt Busby has the same kind of considerate nature. Once, at an international match, he ticked me off for not going to a reception in the directors' room. I told him that I felt overawed by the others there and he ticked me off again. 'Never forget that in your sons you have something they can never have and all their money can never buy for them,' he said.

After that I was never self-conscious about being a pitman's wife, no matter how high-flown the company.

And on 30 July 1966 the company couldn't have been more high flown. The Queen was there to present the Jules Rimet trophy to the winning team. The Prime Minister, Harold Wilson, was also at the ground.

Later, at a government reception for the victorious England team and their guests, I met Mr Wilson and he demanded to know: 'Why didn't you have a whole team like Bobby and Jack.' I should have told him that it had nearly been done - by my granddad, Old Warhorse.

I had travelled down to London with Bob the day before the big game. We caught the noon train from Central Station, Newcastle and arrived at Kings Cross to be met by massed ranks of photographers and reporters. From the station we were taken to a studio for a live broadcast to the Midlands by Granada Television and then to the Royal Garden Hotel where we had been booked along with England's other official guests.

Royal indeed! The dinner laid on for us that night was fit for a king and certainly luxury indeed for someone who could still vividly recall standing in a soup kitchen queue for a piece of bread and some watery broth. My dinner this time was smoked salmon and chicken, superbly cooked and followed by the most luscious display of sweets I had ever seen.

The morning of the big game was spent with the editor and staff of the *People* newspaper. Then I went out with a photogra-

We had the time of our lives in London after the World Cup final and even talked to Prime Minister Harold Wilson.

pher to have my picture taken buying a hat for the big occasion.

Just after one fifteen p.m., as we travelled up Olympic Way on route to Wembley, I was very proud to be English and to be there for that great, final game. I felt that even if we were beaten, it could hardly have spoiled that amazing day because England would still have been part of the greatest final in the World's greatest football competition.

The only disappointment for me on that lovely day was that my constant companion during so many other games was missing; Jack's wife Pat. Pat was unable to make it to the final because the match was held on the very day she was due to have a baby.

In fact the new addition to the family took another week to put in an appearance, but who knows what might have happened if Pat had been at Wembley in that highly charged atmosphere? Still, I was upset that Pat was not with me as usual, to share the moments which followed.

When we arrived at Wembley I had to rush for a television

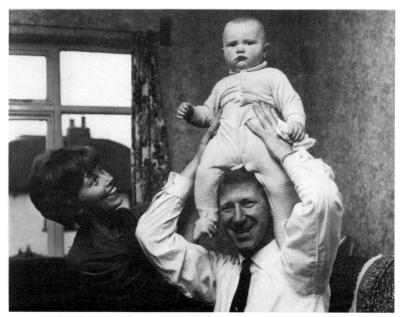

Jack and Pat's third child, Peter – nick-named 'World Cup Willie' because he was due to be born on the day of the World Cup final. As it was – he was a week late.

interview with David Coleman, Billy Wright and Joe Mercer, before I could settle down for the kick-off.

The game which followed was unforgettable. It was a hard, but clean match and dramatic to the last second.

A total of 700 radio and television reporters at Wembley sent their kick-by-kick accounts around the world as the game progressed. Nowhere was the BBC World Service broadcast on it being monitored more closely than in the purser's room on board the merchant ship MV *Glengyle* as it lolled in the moonlit waters of the East China Sea, thirty miles off Shanghai.

My other son Gordon, was an engineer on board the *Glengyle* and although it was eleven p.m. local time, he was unable to listen to the broadcast.

The game clashed with his engine-room shift so he and his shipmates on the same shift had to work in an agony of suspense. They had to rely on other crewmen to relay progress reports and sometimes they were very salty accounts indeed!

Just fifteen seconds before the full-time whistle England lost their 2-1 lead when a free-kick was awarded against Jack for 'climbing' up Held's back to head a ball clear. From the free kick Weber managed to score and it seemed that by his action Jack had pulled England back from the brink of victory.

On board the *Glengyle*, Gordon's heart dropped like a stone when one of the crewmen came down to yell at him, 'That bastard brother of yours has given a goal away!'

But losing the lead didn't mean losing the match. After 30 minutes of extra time the game ended with a 4-2 score in England's favour.

Jack sank to his knees and pressed his forehead into the Wembley turf. Bobby burst into tears and, up in the press box so did I – on Kenneth Wolstenholme's shoulder. He had been the first to congratulate me and we just hugged and hugged each other. The players' wives were a bit pussy-struck by our performance, but we were old friends and it was an emotional moment. I

Although Gordon missed all the excitement of the match, he was able to catch up with it on film when he got home.

had been supposed to do another television interview, but I had to leave and find a quiet corner among all that madness to compose myself instead.

On the *Glengyle*, Gordon's shift ended and along with the other duty men, he climbed to the upper decks, still not knowing the final result. Just before they reached the purser's room, however, the outcome, if not the score, became obvious. Only an England victory could be responsible for the sight in the companionway ahead of them: the strange, and somehow, unnerving sight of their usually remote and imposing captain, J.K. Edmunds, windmilling his arms and legs through a what was meant to pass for a jig.

Gordon later told me that across the temperate waters of that oriental ocean a new sound also filled the warm air that night. One by one, British ships began to sound their sirens until all were chorusing their congratulations. It was an intensely emotional time and one which didn't end with the final whistle. An hour later hardly any of the 93,000 fans packing Wembley had left the ground. They stayed on, enjoying the sweet taste of that English victory for as long as they could. Even when we eventually left the ground we didn't leave that atmosphere behind.

The route to the Royal Garden Hotel was lined with cheering crowds. Outside the Royal Garden, 6,000 more people awaited the return of England's victors. The players followed us in and after a quick change we met in the Bulldog Bar for a cocktail party before the official banquet. So many people crammed into the bar that it was like the Black Hole of Calcutta. The difference here was that the 'victims' were willing, in fact eager, to be there.

Those 'victims' included Prime Minister, Harold Wilson, his Cabinet colleagues, George Brown and Jim Callaghan, as well as players from all the competing teams.

I escaped from the crush to be shown the Royal Garden's Banqueting Room by the manager before it was invaded by celebrators. What a sight. So many flags and flowers; so much fine silver and so much polishing for some poor soul to do!

As I admired the displays, two players from the defeated West German team came in and very gallantly gave me gifts. One presented his tie-pin to me and the other offered his buttonhole.

Lavish meals awaited players and official guests and throughout the whole of the banquet a cheering, chanting crowd outside the hotel kept up their cries of 'England, England' and 'Charlton, Charlton'. Later I joined the team to wave from a hotel balcony. Bob went off to bed at eleven thirty p.m., but I stayed up until two a.m. and even at that late hour the crowds were still chanting and dancing.

What a day – what a night!

The day after that history-making game, the team and their guests met again. We all went to Wardour Street to see Pathe Gazette's edited film of the final and then had more interviews, this time with the foreign press. Everyone was still elated and Jack showed it by some typical mickey-taking when we all went for lunch.

His fellow defender George Cohen became the butt of Jack's jokes. Jack wanted to know about George's Jewish background. 'I'm not Jewish', George replied.

Jack turned to me, on his other side, and said loudly 'George says he's not Jewish but he must be with a name like that.' Once poor George had risen to the bait Jack played him like a prize fish. He wouldn't let up teasing him until George finally leaped to his feet, grabbed his fly zip and yelled: 'Come outside Jack and I'll prove that I'm not Jewish.' Jack just hooted and let George off the hook.

We had wined and dined on the best that weekend, but by then, all Jack wanted was some plain cooking. After three weeks on hotel food, he'd had enough, even if it was the best.

As he drove me away from London Jack declared that he just had to have some fried egg and chips and stopped at the first transport cafe we reached. Only when he had downed a double helping of eggs and chips could we finally head for home.

148

CHAPTER FIFTEEN

A week after those unforgettable events at Wembley, Pat presented Jack with another memento of the occasion – a second son, Peter James Charlton.

Although Peter and Pat missed out on the World Cup final, they were around for one very special celebration which followed in its wake, on 17 August.

Civic leaders in Ashington decided that it was about time they paid their own tribute to two home-grown sporting heroes by arranging a town hall reception and banquet in honour of Bobby and Jack. What a day that was!

The event was meant to 'kick off' with a procession starting from outside my home in Beatrice Street at six fifteen in the evening. But that official starting time was ignored by many people. They began to congregate in the back lane from first thing in the morning. Colourful bunting had been strung across the narrow street overnight. Posters, banners and flags were fastened to the high, yellow brick wall enclosing ours and neighbouring back yards.

By ten a.m. children were beginning to gather outside my house and chatter excitedly. Youngsters who had climbed onto wall tops outside our house, as the day progressed, set up a cheer which was caught and echoed by several hundred people in the street below everytime one of us came to the door. It was flattering - but also embarrassing. Our only toilet stood at the bottom of the yard and anyone using it had to do so with several well-wishers clumping around on the roof over their head.

At five p.m. the back lane was filled with a surging mass of people. Youngsters were standing on each others' shoulders to scramble onto the top of our yard wall in an effort to catch a glimpse of Bobby or Jack. By that time Jack and Pat had arrived with their children, Deborah, John and little Peter in his carry-cot.

149

What a welcome! Ashington went wild as its two sons came home for a reception after their World Cup victory in August 1966.

Yellow Rolls Royce owner Donald Heyworth, chauffeurs the boys from Beatrice Street to the reception.

The Yellow Rolls Royce is swamped in a sea of well-wishers at the entrance to Ashington Town Hall.

Council Chairman, Tom Harkness with Jack and Bobby at the civic reception.

Police were called to help control the crowds now jamming the back lane. But there was no sign of Bobby and Norma. Jack was getting really worried.

Lancashire industrialist Donald Heyworth had read of the civic reception idea in a newspaper and offered to drive Bobby and Jack the half-mile to Ashington's town hall in his 1926 open-top yellow Rolls Royce. We were beginning to think that Jack would be making the journey on his own when Bobby and Norma finally turned up. He said that they had been in the town for some time and had tried to come to Beatrice Street earlier in the day, but when he saw the size of the crowd already filling the lane, they sought refuge with my cousin Chuck Charlton, who lived nearby at North Seaton, until it was almost time to leave.

When that moment came, Bobby slipped in through our little-used front door and straight out through the back where Mr Heyworth and his Rolls Royce were waiting. The street was an amazing sight that day, people were crammed shoulder to shoulder and from among that sea of well-wishers banners sprouted and on them, the message 'Bobby and Jack – a credit to Ashington'.

I wonder what old Warhorse would have made of that. By all the evidence the 'Milburn strain' was alive and kicking better than ever under the Charlton mantle!

It was a terrific struggle, but first Bobby and Jack, then Bob and me along with their wives, heaved ourselves through the crowd of noisy well-wishers to our waiting cars. Minutes earlier it had begun to rain, but no one seemed to notice or to care.

Jack made the most of that half-mile trip, perched there on the back of the rear seat. He waved and grinned all the way to the town hall, every inch of which was lined by cheering people.

Bobby, as usual, looked worried and distinctly uncomfortable. From the press of bodies a young boy of about ten darted in front of the Rolls Royce. 'Shake me hand. Shake me hand', he begged. Bobby was desperately worried that the boy might slip under the wheels of Mr Heyworth's car and eventually he leaned danger-ously far out to oblige him.

Ashington's population in 1966 was just under 30,000 and it

seemed as if the whole town had turned out, in the rain, to salute the lads. Led by Ashington Colliery brass band the procession made its way through the town centre to the strains of Sousa while the crowd sang 'When the Saints Go Marching In.'

Outside the town hall, live-broadcast television cameras were pointed towards the approaching procession. A floor manager was almost trampled underfoot, caught in a sudden surge of cheering well-wishers. When the motorcade stopped outside the town hall it was immediately surrounded by thousands of people who did to the town centre's main road what we had already witnessed in Beatrice Street.

Ashington town centre had been sealed off to traffic, which was just as well, because the cheering crowds had it blocked solid.

Bobby and Jack managed, with difficulty, to climb out of the Rolls Royce leaving behind an elated Mr Heyworth waving a football over his head in a two handed salute.

Bob and me, in the following car, had just as difficult a job to walk the few paces from the kerbside to the council steps. Like Bobby and Jack, we too had to be escorted by police through that surging crush of people. It was a scary experience.

Inside the council chamber council chairman Tom Harkness formally welcomed us and presented Bobby and Jack with inscribed watches and silver tankards. Jack immediately slipped on his watch then produced his World Cup winners medal. In the glare of the television lights it gleamed brilliantly.

This was a unique occasion, yet it still reminded me of days gone by, for the town hall stands on Station Bridge in the centre of town, the same bridge which, a generation earlier, the Milburn clan, including little Cis, crossed on their way to collect their sports day rewards at Paddy Mullen's drapery shop. Half a century later and just yards from the same spot, it was now the turn of my own two sons to repeat the process on a much grander scale.

After the official presentations we left for a banquet at Ashington's Hirst Welfare Miners' Hall. But getting there was no easier than when we made the journey to the town hall. The thousands who had turned out to welcome Bobby and Jack as they arrived, were still there in force when we tried to leave and, in fact, our departure was even more chaotic than our arrival. Somehow, instead of getting into the official car, Jack charged into one driven by a reporter, Vince Gledhill. Rather than return to the mêlée to await the official transport, they set off for Hirst Welfare in Vince's old Triumph Herald. Following close behind them was Roy Nuttall, Ashington's town clerk and the man whose carefully-laid plans for this highly-publicised event seemed to be going off course.

Half-way to the Welfare his worst fears seemed to be taking shape before his eyes. Inside the Triumph Herald Jack was shouting, 'Stop! Stop the car!' The cavalcade behind them also slowed as the Herald braked. A mystified Roy Nuttall watched Jack climb out of the car and head for a workingmen's club a few yards away.

Jack had taken it into his head to pop in for a pint and see some

While the grown-ups enjoyed the civic reception, Jack's bairns John and Debbie (front, seated) tucked in at a street party in Beatrice Street.

of his old mates, regardless of the fact that a banquet organised in his honour would have to be held up until he arrived. Red-faced Roy jumped from his car and ran to the club doorway barring Jack's path. It says something for his powers of persuasion that he talked Jack into getting back into the car. Jack has never been one to change his mind after deciding to do something.

However, we did eventually all arrive at the welfare and the celebrations continued.

There were many tributes paid to my sons in that year of 1966, but I do know that they felt this one to be special. None of us had expected anything like it, and I know that the lads were very touched by it.

The World Cup and the fuss that followed it pushed us all even further into the limelight than we had been before. It definitely changed our lives and made us feel even more as if we were living in a goldfish bowl at Beatrice Street. But I was still taken by surprise when Jack came to me the day after the civic reception and announced, 'I've bought you a house Mam.'

I was hanging out my washing at the time. I stopped pegging and said, 'You haven't!'

'I have,' he answered. 'Do you want it?'

'Oh yes,' I replied.

The house was on a new estate at College Road, Ashington. It had been built on part of Wembley field, the same field where I had played as a bairn and, during the 1926 strike watched the pitch and toss gamblers.

Jack had been asked to officially open a show house on the estate. He liked it so much that while performing the opening ceremony, he announced that he was going to buy one for Bob and me. Just before the speech, Pat had agreed with him that we would probably like to have one of these nice new houses. But she was still taken aback when he announced the decision in such a public way. The house cost £2,700 and reports at the time suggested that Jack had bought it from his World Cup winnings. In fact his winnings amounted to £1,400 which dropped to less than £1,000 after the taxman had taken his cut.

As I stood open-mouthed in Beatrice Street, after he dropped the bombshell news, Jack said, 'Come on, leave the washing and put your coat on. Come and see which one you want.'

We dragged Bob from his bed to go with us and choose our new home. The house we picked was number eight, College Road. We decided to call it Jules Rimet, after the World Cup trophy. It seemed a fitting name.

I had walked many times past the estate where our new home stood and thought how nice it must be to end your days in a comfortable, modern home like one of these and here we were about to move into one. I was so excited.

In Beatrice Street we had a lot of good neighbours, but the houses lacked amenities which are nowadays regarded as basic. Although the year was 1966 we still had no bathroom; washing and cooking were both done in the walk-in pantry; the toilet and coalhouse were still at the bottom of the yard and the open coal fire had to heat the whole house.

Jules Rimet had three bedrooms, an indoor bathroom and **toilet, a fitted kitchen, a dining room and a lounge. They were**

Bob and me outside Jules Rimet, our house which never quite became a home.

156

luxuries we could never have afforded and never expected to enjoy.

Yet for all the comforts of Jules Rimet it never became home. I never succeeded in settling down there. I found that I had exchanged the sharing happiness of a working-class atmosphere for middle-class estate snobbery. One day I heard some women talking about me. 'Fancy, she's moving into that house and she doesn't even have fitted carpets', one of them said.

The thought of someone thinking that they were God-knows-what just because they had bought a new house and some bits of new furniture was too much for me. Although we were thrilled to have this new house which undoubtedly made our lives more comfortable, old-fashioned Beatrice Street was still where our hearts called home.

Even our mongrel dog Chuck turned up his nose at the new house. He just couldn't get used to it. As soon as he was allowed outside, he bounded over the fence and turned tail for Beatrice Street. His days were spent scrounging scraps of food from former neighbours before reluctantly wandering back home at night.

Although we had a nice, new house and I was well used to press people calling, I just wasn't in the mood for entertaining when Jack told me that Clement (now Sir Clement) Freud wanted to interview me for a feature he was writing. 'Can't I meet him somewhere, aah'm just not in the fettle for cookin' for another reporter,' I said. The answer came back later that we were to meet for lunch at the Royal Station Hotel in Newcastle. When the day came round, I was quite looking forward to the date and in preparation for it I didn't eat much for breakfast.

We met at the hotel and, in spite of his famous hangdog expression, Clement was anything but dour company. He was, however, very fussy about the meal we had. I ordered steak and asked for a medium rare one. Clement had liver, bacon and onions and the smell from the kitchen had my mouth watering as we talked.

When our meal arrived the waiter was carefully placing mine in front of me when Clement gave it a disapproving glare. 'That's not medium rare, take it away,' he ordered. My heart sank. It looked alright to me – and I was so hungry.

A short while later, the waiter came back and once again a steaming steak, with all the trimmings, was placed in front of me – only to fail the Freud test yet again.

I was famished by now and I there was a limit to how fussy my stomach would allow me to be. When the next steak arrived, the plate had hardly touched the table when I whipped up my fork and stabbed it down – hard!

'That'll do very nicely, thankyou,' I said to the waiter. Clement got the message. At last we began to eat – and how delicious it was!

Bob and I lived in our College Road home for six years. During that time he was made redundant from the pits and I got myself a job at Hepworth's tailoring factory in Ashington. There, among the factory girls, I found some of the companionship I had lost by moving from Beatrice Street.

Then, when Bob and me were both retired, Jack came up with another surprise. He asked us to lift up our roots completely this time and leave Ashington for good.

CHAPTER 16

Mornings were the worst for Bob. He had suffered from pneumo-
coniosis, the miners' dust disease, since he was forty and it had
left him with congested lungs which rattled on damp mornings or
in smoke-filled atmospheres. So when Jack asked us to go down
to Carleton village, in the West Riding of Yorkshire, where he had
bought a farmhouse, I thought that all that healthy, moorland air
would be just the thing for Bob.

We spent a few weekends at the farmhouse first and Bob loved
it. After a lifetime of working hard in a lightless hole under the
ground this was real luxury for him.

The farm stands at the end of a private road with a pretty copse
and a burn nearby. At the front of the house is a large garden with
an uninterrupted view across to the other side of the valley.

At the back of the house lie the Carleton Moors full of grouse
and very popular with shooting parties.

It was for us a perfect setting; peaceful and splendid with a
rugged Yorkshire beauty and couldn't have offered a more different way of life to the one we had known in our close-knit pit town.

When Jack asked us to move into permanently and look after
the farm for him, we grabbed his offer with hardly a second's
thought. Who wouldn't have?

Bob made an immediate impression on the farm and on
Carleton's little community and we struck up a friendship with
the people living on the next farm, Ray and Vera Hunter. Bob
liked nothing better than helping Ray around his farm and I found
a lasting friend in Vera. Their children, Valerie and Andrew,
called me Granny and I loved to hear them say it.

At the side of Jack's farm was a small garden which Bob
claimed as his allotment patch. On that little scrap of land he
raised pigeons and hens as well as vegetables for my kitchen.

Bantam hens are very popular on allotments in pit towns like

Ashington, and Bob was especially proud of his birds at Carleton, particularly his bantam cockerel. It really was a magnificent sight as it strutted around the farm, its glossy feathers gleaming in the sunlight – so proud, so cocksure and literally ruling the roost.

Together Bob and I also planted hundreds of daffodil bulbs and gladioli around the place and when they flowered it was a riot of colour.

We spent many hours sitting at the front of the house on a wooden seat which Bob had made, admiring the beauty of our surroundings. But I must admit that the seat on which we sat was less than beautiful. It had been made by Bob in his own very special fashion – a fashion which owed more to pit-town allotment cree carpentry than the Reader's Digest Do-It-Yourself manual.

The seat was an old door laid on its side with two supporting legs and a back rest hammered on to it with the usual six-inch nails!

In all his many years of allotment work Bob never willingly bought a piece of wood or a nail. He scavenged timber from anywhere, first yanking out any old nails he could find in it, then hammering them straight ready to use again.

On the other hand, despite its looks, that garden seat did stand the test of time, as did the chicken cree and the greenhouse that Bob also built.

The greenhouse was made from old window frames which he had bought from a man in the village for £4. But to be fair, when Bob finished building it, that greenhouse was as solid as a rock. As Jack said afterwards: 'Only a greenhouse built by me Faatha would stand up to the sort of winds we get here.'

Bob's success with hammer and saw were no use to him when it came to his goat, however. I never knew what scheme Bob was going to come up with next, but he still took me aback when he announced that he was going to get a goat. He didn't know the first thing about goatkeeping, but the more he thought about it, the better the idea sounded. A goat would save him from having to mow the lawn outside the farmhouse and provide us with fresh, free, milk, he said.

I could see that the idea had taken root and nothing I could say would change his mind. Soon after his announcement Bob bought himself a nanny.

His first mistake was in taking delivery of the goat with its udder already full. His second was in assuming that any fool can milk a goat. Some can't!

As soon as he got it home Bob set about trying to relieve the goat of its straining load. He planted a three-legged stool beside the uncomfortable animal and then parked himself on it. But what an odd sight he made, perched there on that tiny stool.

Our son Gordon was visiting us on that particular day. I turned to him and said: 'Eee son, yer dad looks just like an Anderson's pork sandwich.'

I should explain that Anderson's is a pork butchers shop in Ashington where the sandwiches it sold were famous for having so much meat in them that a large part of the filling always hung over the edge of the bun – just like Bob's ample backside overlapping the little milking stool.

He tried and tried to coax milk from the goat's swollen udder; the goat, was obviously just as anxious to be relieved of her burden. But somehow they just couldn't manage to co-ordinate their efforts. I offered to try as well, but I knew even less about goats than Bob. Eventually we sent for Vera from the farm next door. But by that time the poor goat had had enough. She was sore and sick of us messing her around so even Vera couldn't manage to milk her.

Bob had a fiery temper and by this time his short fuse had already burnt down to the explosive. Gordon and I waited for the 'bang' that was bound to come. When it did arrive, Bob picked up his empty milking jug and hurled it as far as he could, smashing it to smithereens.

The sound and the fury of Bob's tantrum terrified the goat so much that she took off across the field making a beeline for her old home and sanctuary. Bob, red-faced, yelling with frustration and anger, took off after her and caught the goat by a boundary wall. Then he hauled the poor creature back across the field and headed towards our car with her.

161

Furiously he yanked open one of the doors and pushed the goat on to the passenger seat, then he planted himself in the driver's seat and chauffeured the bewildered beast back to its original owner who, fortunately, agreed to take her back.

Bob wasn't the only one whose business ideas went astray. Jack had a plan for rearing his own pheasants at Carleton, but that was another scheme which failed to hatch. He bought all the equipment for incubating the eggs, but only a handful of them hatched. We learned afterwards that because the breed stock had been given water at the wrong time it had made the birds lay eggs with shells too tough for the chicks to break through.

Pheasant and grouse-shooting was a popular and profitable pastime in that part of the world. American visitors were known to pay dearly for the right to shoot on the moors beside our farm. It also became a tradition on the 12th August for us to hold a 'Game Party' at the farm for the beaters and shooters who went out with Jack on the moors. As many as we could put up arrived the night before the 12th and the next day their wives usually arrived while the men were on the moors. At first we had 20 to 25 guests, but as word about the 'Game Parties' spread, the number had climbed to 50 by the time we decided that it was just too many for me to cater for. But they were smashing days before they got out of hand.

In the morning, while the men were out shooting, the women went shopping, usually in Northallerton, and later they would go to Braithwaite Hall, where their men were shooting and pick up the grouse for me to cook for the night-time.

In spite of the birds, though, it was my rabbit pies which were the most popular dish of those days. I had a special recipe which always had them coming back for more. 'Why on earth don't my rabbit pies taste like that?' I was asked many times. The secret was in my special 'gravy'. After cooking all the other meats and poultry, the venison, the grouse, the pork, beef, pigeon and geese, I blended together all the stock from them which then went into the 'rabbit' pie. No wonder it had such a special flavour!

After the evening meal, when we were all relaxed and in good humour, the night usually ended with home entertainment. We all took a turn, but Jack's party piece always brought the house down.

To perform it he climbs onto a chair and slowly sinks into a crouch. He draws his hands up his sides until those bony elbows of his stick straight out. He first lowers his head and then, slowly, with that long neck of his stretching as far as he can make it, he lifts his eyes to the ceiling and begins to flap his arms. With those gangling limbs, craning neck and hairless pate, that is Jack's perfectly hilarious imitation of – an American bald eagle!

Jack's love of shooting and country sports has sometimes seemed to put him at odds with his openly socialist opinions. He has been shooting with members of the Royal Family and the aristocracy. On the other hand, another of Jack's friends is National Union of Mineworkers' president, Arthur Scargill. Arthur and Jack became friendly when they lived near each other at Barnsley. Considering their mining backgrounds and outspoken ways it would have been more of a surprise if they hadn't hit it off.

Bob loved those days in the Yorkshire countryside; the fishing, the shooting, the hare-chasing with his whippet Bonnie and the daily stroll with her down to his new local, The Foresters, in Carleton village. For Bob those days were all that retirement is meant to be and for me too they were happy times. I have always been a good mixer at my best with a lot of people around me. I suppose it comes from my being part of a large family and being raised in a close-knit community like Ashington.

Moving to somewhere as isolated as Carleton could have given me problems considering that background. The fact that it didn't was largely due to the way we and our neighbours, the Hunters, 'adopted' each other. We became more like family than friends.

Jack also paid us regular visits with Pat and their children and those visits were always lively. Jack and Bob argued as they always had, but Pat and I had learned long before that it was just their way with each other.

Once, when we were living in College Road, a television team came to the house to make a programme called Big Jack's Other

Jack, at the end of his playing career in 1972 could never resist a kick around. (*The Sun*)

World. They filmed me making Sunday lunch and as I served it up Bob and Jack even began to row about the best way to carve the Sunday joint. I squirmed as they squabbled and the cameras rolled. But they didn't give a damn.

It had been just the same earlier in the programme when the cameras followed Bob and Jack down to Bob's allotment garden and Jack ribbed him about building his pigeon cree with six-inch nails.

In 1973, just a few months before that programme was made, Jack reached the end of his playing career after 23 years with Leeds United. It had been a career filled with controversy – and courage.

Jack's technique of positioning himself on the opposing team's goal-line, where his power and giraffe neck was a constant and unsettling threat to defenders, often paid dividends, but also made him a prime target for off-the-ball play and doubtful refereeing.

In an interview with Brian Glanville of the *Sunday Times*, Jack complained that referees were 95 percent for goalkeepers and five

164

percent for him in any clash. He said: 'I've been pushed in the back, kicked in the back, climbed on top of by defenders and held by both arms and I've never been given a foul.'

He really upset a lot of people in the game when he said in one television interview that he had a 'little black book' containing the names of those players who had hacked him and he planned to make sure that they would be on the receiving end the next time he played against them. He was only saying aloud what most players were saying to themselves, but the powers-that-be didn't see it that way and accused him of bringing the game into disrepute.

Jack had thought that with the end of his playing days he would make a clean break from soccer. But things didn't work out that way. He was invited to manage Middlesborough at the end of the 1972-73 season and decided to give it a try.

He soon found that being the boss called for a whole new set of skills. He suddenly discovered that instead of openly voicing his opinions and criticisms, he was expected to play the diplomat, coaxing and cajoling on the playing field and in the boardroom to manoeuvre others round to his way of thinking.

Jack hated the idea of having to be devious, so in his early days at Middlesborough he made it clear to everyone there that he would not tolerate whispering campaigns or cliques. Problems and grievances should be brought out into the open and not allowed to fester, he ordered. Neither did he care much for players whose main reason for being in the game was money. He believed in a socialist system in which all players are paid the same and never need to ask for a rise.

In 1974 Middlesborough returned to Division One for the first time in twenty years, securing their place there with a 1-0 victory over Oxford and a record points total. By 1976 they were third from top. In November the same year Jack went to Buckingham Palace to collect an O.B.E. for his services to football.

In 1977 he took over as manager of Sheffield Wednesday and saw the team promoted twice during his four years in charge. However, his abrasive manner was not always appreciated by the fans, something which years later also led to him dramatically walking out on Newcastle United.

In the same year that Jack's playing career ended, Bobby also hung up his boots. In a long and distinguished playing career with Manchester United, lasting twenty years, he had scored 192 goals in 570 league appearances. He had also won all of the game's major honours including winners' medals for the World Cup, the European Cup, the League Championship and the FA Cup. He had been capped for England 106 times and scored 49 goals in the process. Bobby was awarded an O.B.E. in 1969 for his services to the sport and in 1973 received a C.B.E.

More than any other footballer of his time he was known throughout the World as an ambassador for the English way of football. His name became a byword for integrity and skill on the field of play and for his testimonial match 61,000 fans squeezed into Old Trafford to show their appreciation for his contribution to the sport.

Bobby's number one fan Barbara Cartland and me. We sat together at lunch and got on like a house on fire. (© D. C. Thomson & Co. Ltd.)

He left Manchester United in April 1973 and a month later became manager of Preston North End. Two years later, Bobby resigned in protest at the board of directors' decision to transfer John Bird to Newcastle United. After resigning, Bobby concentrated more on his business interests, including a travel agency in Hale Barnes, Cheshire, near his home in Knutsford.

In 1975, the year Bobby parted company with Preston North End, I was invited to London to lunch at Claridges with a group of women who all had famous sons and daughters. It was a publicity stunt dreamed up by a firm which makes Mothers Day cards and it sounded like a laugh, so I accepted the invitation and took my neighbour Vera Hunter with me.

It was the first time Vera had been to London, so after lunching at Claridges we took a taxi trip around the city, heading first for Buckingham Palace. Our driver turned out to be from Sunderland and the sound of my North East accent made him nostalgic. Every time I stopped talking he demanded: 'Say some more, keep talking!' He must have switched off his meter as well, because the cost of taking us around the city came to just £1.50.

While I had been at Claridges having my photograph taken with a group of mothers whose sons and daughters included, Tom Jones, Jimmy Tarbuck, Barbara Windsor, John Conteh, Peter Oosterhuis, Brendan Foster and Virginia Wade, I saw another unmistakeable face.

Barbara Cartland, writer of so many popular romantic novels swept across to me and announced that she was a big fan of Bobby Charlton. 'Every time he is on the television my daughters tell me to come and watch my boyfriend,' she said and suggested that we should have our photograph taken together.

By the 1980s our other two sons, Gordon and Tommy, had completed their own families and were settled in their careers. Gordon and his wife, Jenny, had Brett and Kellie. Tommy and his wife Carol had Andrew, John and Lisa, who was born in 1982. Gordon is a director in a firm producing specialist handmade fireplaces in Barnsley and Tommy became an officer in the Mines Rescue Brigade; he was based first in Scotland and later in Yorkshire.

He could be infuriating, but Bob could always make me laugh.

In 1984 Bobby was asked back to Manchester United – this time as a director of the club.

In our Carleton home, Bob and me were never lonely, despite its isolation. Bob had a way, when there was no-one else around, of filling the place with just his presence. He embarrassed me, he annoyed me, he argued just for the sake of argument. But after all our years together he could still surprise me and still make me laugh. So the time in Carleton seemed to fly for the two of us. No sooner had the summer arrived than winter was back on the doorstep.

Bob and I always spent Christmas at Jack's other home in Barnsley. Christmas 1981 was no exception. But this time as we left the farmhouse which had been our home for the previous nine years, it was for the last time together. Bob had been complaining of dizziness, but his GP told him that it was simply 'old age' and he would just have to grin and bear it.

Before going to Jack's that Christmas, we called in on Gordon at Leeds for a few days. When he saw his father, Gordon insisted on taking him to another doctor. Gordon's doctor said that Bob was suffering from anaemia and prostate trouble and had him admitted to St. James' hospital in Leeds immediately.

At St. James, Bob was given a blood transfusion and doctors carried out a series of tests. What they found was that he had cancer. A few days later he was allowed out in time for Christmas at Jack's, but while he was there he suffered a heart attack and was rushed to Hallamshire Hospital in Sheffield. Later he was pronounced well enough to travel back to St James for more tests. From there he was moved to Cookridge Hospital in Leeds.

In April 1982 my Bob, the kid with the half-moon grin, the dance-hall beau on the rebound, the bold young buck whose boxing booth battle won the wedding ring I still wear, lost his last fight. He died, aged seventy two, at Cookridge Hospital and was cremated at Lawnswood Crematorium in Leeds.

After Bob's death I didn't know what to do with myself. Eventually I told Jack and Gordon that I wanted to go back to the farm to see if I could manage on my own. I have always had an independent nature and I was determined to cope without leaning on the lads.

I managed quite well from April until July and thought that I was going to be able to go on living there. Occasionally I received a painful reminder of happier times as on the day I got a call from Bob's old local, the Foresters. The landlord said that our whippet Bonnie had made her own way down to the pub, climbed into Bob's usual seat and was refusing to budge from it. That was a rough moment, but I coped.

Then in July I went out as usual to feed the hens. They had proved to be one of Bob's successful ventures and I decided to keep them on. But that summer morning I made a discovery which brought all of the heartbreak of the past months to a head. I found Bob's bantam cockerel dead.

It was a beautiful creature, especially when the sun shone on its brilliant feathers and Bob had been so proud of it. As I stood looking at that dead bird lying in the cree which Bob had built, I realised that I couldn't bear to bury it and neither could I stay at the farm.

169

We'd had so much happiness there that it was too painful to stay and watch reminders of what we'd had fade and die also. Only by getting away would I be able to keep my memories from haunting me.

I decided to go back to Ashington.

CHAPTER SEVENTEEN

When I returned to Ashington in August 1982, I moved into a small council flat. Bob had put our names on the council-house waiting list in 1934 and regularly renewed it ever since. It proved a wise precaution. My former home in College Road hadn't been sold, but it was rented to a young couple and the lease still had a couple of years to run.

Before I left Carleton I found a good home for Bonnie. Our good neighbour, Ray Hunter, offered to call at the farmhouse each morning to feed the hens. He also made me a promise: 'They are Bob's hens and I'll look after them until they die a natural death,' he said.

After almost fifty years of marriage to one man, it came as a terrible blow to lose him and I was worried that settling into a new life back in Ashington, without him, would be an uphill task.

Yet I was surprised to find how easy it was to pick up the threads of my former life in the town. It is often said that going back to old haunts in search of past happiness is a mistake. If that is right, then I have been lucky, because back in the town where I was born and raised my own family, I found support and friendship to help me cope with life without Bob.

I was welcomed back to Ashington with open arms – quite literally. So many old friends stopped me and gave me such lovely cuddles as I walked through the town centre that I couldn't get my shopping done. They were just the tonic I needed.

I lost a big part of my own life when I lost Bob, but the warmth I found when I came back filled some of the emptiness I felt. I regretted why I'd had to come back to Ashington, but never for a minute have I regretted coming back here. It was the best thing I could have done and for as long as I am able to look after myself I am happy to stay where I am.

Independence, you will probably have gathered, is another

family trait!

Early in 1983 rumours began to circulate in the press that Jack Charlton was about to return to the North East as manager of Newcastle United. At the time when the rumours were at their height, Jack and Pat were abroad at their apartment in Spain. I didn't know whether he would take the job because Newcastle's directors had a reputation for meddling in decisions which should be left to the manager and I knew that Jack would never tolerate that.

When they returned from Spain Jack went for talks with United's directors. Afterwards he secretly told me that he was going to take the job, but he refused to sign a contract. He wanted nothing binding him to the club in case things did not work out. When the time did come for him to part company with the club, it would be quick and uncomplicated with no messy rows about contract obligations, he said.

Both Jack and me came back to Ashington within months of each other and it was grand to spend time together again. Jack's love of fishing took us to the Kielder Reservoir to help stock it with fish.

I was over the moon, but keeping that news to myself was agony. I am the world's worst keeper of secrets and I was bursting to tell someone. As ordered, I didn't let the cat out of the bag, but to be honest, I'm sure that the news was written on my face for anyone to read.

When Jack agreed to become Newcastle's new manager, he and Pat were living in Barnsley, not far from Arthur Scargill, as a matter of fact. They had a beautiful home, but decided to sell up and move to the North East. That proved more of a problem than either of them expected. Both Jack and Pat will be the first to admit that they are strong-willed and finding a new home that suited both of them proved nearly as difficult as managing a First Division team. When they left their 17th century house in Barnsley, they still hadn't agreed on a place in the North East.

Both of them had loved the home they were leaving. It stood in 10 acres of land, much of which had been wilderness when they moved in six years earlier. As far as Jack was concerned the challenge of making something of that wilderness with his own hands had been one of the big attractions of the place. With the help of Herbert, their part-time gardener, Jack planted about a thousand trees and shrubs and created a pond stocked with trout at the bottom of an acre of lawn.

He happily spent whole days in the garden chopping wood and scything nettles. Like his father, Bob, he is happiest in the open air doing something which taxes his imagination along with his muscles.

Parting with that place, only added to the pressures on Jack and Pat. He wanted somewhere with as much space around it as he could get while Pat wanted somewhere not too remote from civilisation. Jules Rimet, the house that Jack bought for Bob and me in 1966, provided a temporary solution. When the lease on it came to an end the tenants moved out and Jack and Pat moved in.

The 1984 football season began and, for me, it was almost like returning to the old days. Newcastle was back in the First Division and I never missed a chance to watch them in action. Teammates and opponents from Jack and Bobby's playing days were also at these games as managers, coaches, club officials and commentators. Bobby Robson, Ian Porterfield, Bobby Kerr, Norman Hunter, Maurice Setters, Willie Maddren and, of course, Wor Jackie, my cousin Jack Milburn, who was then a sports reporter for the *News of the World*.

The friends, the atmosphere, the game, they have their ups and downs, but football is still in my blood. I have to admit that at heart I'm still that mudlark bairn wanting to chase a ball across a pit heap or dance to the sound of fiddle and accordian in a colliery row on a summer's night.

As I look back over the years now, I also look forward and wonder how long the Milburn-Charlton strain will have a place in English football. It's been going now for more than a hundred years, since the time when Warhorse Milburn warmed up his iron muscles at the coalface before taking to the football field. If it does show up in the next generation of English footballers, it will not be through Bobby's or Jack's children. Bobby has two daughters, Suzanne and Andrea, and no sons.

Of Jack's two sons, Peter has no fancy for a career in football and although John has a good reputation as a player, he is as far away from English soccer as anyone can get – 16,000 miles actually. He went to live, and play football, in Australia.

If the Milburn streak is to make its mark on this country's next generation of footballers, it might be through my grandsons born to Gordon and Jenny, or Tommy and Carol.

Brett Charlton, Gordon's son, was, at the age of eleven, as enthusiastic about the game as any of the Milburns or Charltons in his family tree. His cousin Andrew, Tommy's eldest son, and two years older than Brett, was the model of Bobby at the same age in his love of the game. He played for a Scottish youth team until he moved to Rotherham when his father transferred to the Mines Rescue station there.

When Bobby was that age he loved to sit by his grandfather Tanner's side and talk about football. Andrew is just the same with me. He likes nothing better than to sit and talk to me for hours about football with that same seriousness which Bobby had when he and Tanner talked.

Once, when I was staying at his house, Andrew confidentially asked me to get up at seven a.m. with him. When I asked why he wanted me up so early, he said, 'So that we can talk about football for a couple of hours before the others get up.' So I got up at seven and we talked, just the two of us, about the game as it was and as it is now. Andrew has so many of Bobby's ways about him that I feel very hopeful for him. I would like to live long enough to see him make the best of his natural skill.

When I talked with Andrew it brought back memories of my own early days of going to matches to watch my heroes. I like to think back to the time when top class wingers like Bobby Mitchell, ruled the pitch. I have always felt that the decision by most of Britain's leading teams to scrap wingers, after 1966, robbed the game of a lot of its excitement. As far as I am concerned, wingers provided the best action of all on the football field, if they did the job right. What they did was pure entertainment. Tom Finney and Eddie Gray were master wingers. Whenever they got a ball they didn't get rid of it straight away. They hung onto the ball all the way upfield, dribbling around opponents, teasing and tantalising them, but never losing possession. They intimidated the opposition by skill, not strength and that always made the game much more exciting. All the same, I also know the weakness of the winger system. They are too vulnerable out on the wing. Blocking a lone winger will always be much easier than stopping a 'pack attack' under the 4-3-3 system. Alf Ramsay realised that when he used the system so successfully in 1966 and England was rewarded with the World Cup. Since then wingers have become a dying breed, but I still believe that football has become less entertaining because of it.

I have to confess that of my four sons, Jack's nature is the closest to my own. He is very straight-talking and doesn't soft-pedal if he thinks I am wrong; while the others would perhaps try to spare my feelings. By the same token I like to have my say too, especially when it involves football.

I told Jack he was wrong to give Peter Beardsley a public dressing down on the pitch at the end of a match late in the 1984-85 season. Jack was angry with what he said was Peter's lack of commitment during the match. The fans didn't like it, neither did

I, and I told him so. 'You should have waited until you were back in the dressing room,' I said.

He explained: 'I just had to get it off my chest,' and I knew what he meant.

Jack was just letting Peter know where he stood with him. Some people appreciate such openness, Peter didn't. Neither did the supporters, and it drove a wedge between them and Jack at a time when he should have been winning their support for his long-term plans to make Newcastle United great again.

Jack's popularity with the fans at St. James' Park fell further when Chris Waddle transferred from Newcastle to Tottenham Hotspur after failing to agree terms for a new contract. The decision caused a new row and Jack was so angry about it that he seriously considered packing in there and then. The fact that after a long search he had only just managed to find a new home in Northumberland helped to persuade him to stay. Even so, Jack and Newcastle United did part company before the first league game of his second season as manager there.

The Ipswich striker Eric Gates was the final straw for the supporters. They were furious when Jack's negotiations with Eric broke down and Eric was signed up by Newcastle United's arch-rival, Sunderland, instead. They showed their dissatisfaction at a pre-season friendly against Sheffield United. Throughout the game a hard core of about 5,000 fans chanted, 'Sack Jack' and 'Charlton must go', among other insults.

Jack had always said that he would only stay with United as long as the fans wanted him there. So, when they called for his resignation, he gave it, typically for him, on the spot.

Although Jack left under a cloud and not the way I had hoped for, I can't say that it took me completely by surprise. From the day he joined Newcastle, I had been uneasy about how things would work out. I was delighted, of course, that he had come back to the North East, but I felt that somehow the job was just not right for him. For one thing, I knew that he hadn't wanted to go into football management again. But when the offer of the Newcastle job came up he decided to give it a go. Even so, he was never comfortable with the job. He had been much happier at Sheffield and Middlesborough.

When Jack took over at Newcastle, Kevin Keegan had just left. Kevin had spent two seasons with Newcastle and had been the the darling of the fans who looked to Jack to find an instant replacement for him.

The fans wanted Jack to go out straight away and buy another big name, even if it got them into debt. But Jack did the exact opposite instead - he put the club on to a better financial footing than it had been for years by not spending. Unfortunately when he did have the money to spend, the right players either weren't on the market, or didn't want to come to Newcastle.

He did get George Riley and Gary Megson, and he wanted Eric Gates as well. But Jack and Eric just couldn't agree a price. It was a pity, but there will be other players for Newcastle.

The fans did not see it that way, however. They wanted a star name for the start of the 1985-86 season, nothing less would do and they told Jack so in their own fashion at that pre-season friendly against Sheffield.

I had been on holiday in Wales with my son Gordon when I heard on the radio that Jack had resigned. I was pleased that his decision had been quick and clean. Many years earlier I had told both Bobby and Jack that when they felt they were coming towards the end of their playing careers, to get out straight away while they were at the top.

'Don't stay until the crowds begin to barrack you,' I told them. 'There is nothing worse than hearing fans barracking someone who has been the best in his day.'

I had my cousin, Jackie Milburn in mind when I said those words. I didn't want to see what happened to him, happen to my sons. I have always been a Newcastle United supporter and watched many a Magpie match in the 1950s when Jackie was playing at his best. In those days he was nothing short of a god to United's fans. Then, when he passed his peak, the fans turned on him. What short memories they have!

I listened to what they were saying about Jackie Milburn and it hurt me to hear it. It is sad how soon supporters forget the good things players have achieved and want them kicked out. They did it with 'Wor Jackie' and they were trying to do it with my Jack.

He was out of football for six months and apparently happy to be away from that particular firing line when the rumours began to fly again in the sporting press. This time, Jack was being linked with the Republic of Ireland's national team, which was looking for a new boss.

He was offered the job and, after some careful consideration, agreed to take it.

The appointment caused yet another stir in football circles. George Best certainly didn't welcome the news. On television, George said that the choice of Jack as the first non-Irishman to manage the national side was a mistake. Jack didn't have enough dedication to the game and spent far too much time on other interests away from the football field, George added.

But George, and a lot of other people who judged Jack by opinions instead of results, were made to eat their words late in 1987 when, under Jack's guidance, the team won through to the 1988 European Cup Championships in Germany.

I was delighted for Jack and those hard-working lads on the Republic team, but nothing is ever straightforward in this life. The draw for the contest put the Republic of Ireland up against England – so where should my loyalties lie – with my son or with my country?

Well, I discovered the answer to that question on June 12th 1988, when Jack's lads met England on a sun-soaked pitch in Stuttgart, West Germany. And what I found was that in spite of a lifetime of supporting England – celebrating their victories, sharing their misery in defeat – when it comes to the crunch, blood is still thicker than water.

Sorry England; after all these years, I never thought I would shout for any national side other than my own, but my real loyalty lies with my family.

So when Ray Houghton – man of that match as far as I am concerned – scored the only goal of the game in the sixth minute, I found myself cheering for the boys in green. It was all the more pleasing to see them do so well because they had been rated rank outsiders and very much the underdogs against England, who the bookmakers made joint second favourites to win the championship.

I was thrilled, not just for Jack and the Republic's hardworking team, but for the people they were representing. This time, here was good news about Irish achievement and success hitting the headlines and filling our television screens instead of more bad news about political problems.

I was so proud of what Jack had done in building up and guiding the Republic squad to their success in that marvellous game.

Jack has always insisted that, at the end of the day, any game of football still just boils down to eleven men against eleven men, but I must admit that I had more hope than confidence that they would pull it off. That confidence grew further in the next round of the championships when the Republic held the USSR team to a 1-1 draw.

Even when the Republic was knocked out of the contest by Holland, who scored a solitary (and clearly offside) goal, they lost no face in defeat. They had shown courage, determination and skill and the 250,000 jubilant Irishmen who welcomed them back to Dublin proved that they had given the fans a contest they will always remember, even if the winner's trophy didn't come home with them.

Jack's reward was to be made an 'honorary Irishman' by Charles Haughey, President of the Republic, who said it was the nearest he could come to knighting him and added that the technicality that Jack was still breathing was all that prevented him from being St. Jack as far as the Republic's football fans were concerned.

Jack had given his best advice to the Repulic team; those young lads gave every scrap of energy and ability that they possessed and together they made a little bit of football history. Warhorse would have been proud of them all!

Something else happened as I watched that first game, the one between England and the Republic. Although I still enjoy watching football, I thought that my days of getting emotional about the game were over. After all, I was seventy-five years old by then and I had seen an awful lot of goals cross the line. But sitting in my flat watching that match and aching to hear the final whistle blow before England could score, I realised that the old thrill was back with me once more and as strong as ever. It felt as if I was starting out all over again. But, perhaps it's just that I've never really stopped!

EPILOGUE

One friend who had stayed in touch with me since those long off days when we lived in our colliery house at Beatrice Street, was Margaret Evans. I had known Margaret since she was a girl dating the boy who lived next door to us. Later she moved into the house next door to our Jules Rimet home in College Road. By then Margaret had married and was herself a mother with two children.

After Bob and me moved to Carleton, Margaret occasionally visited us along with her husband, Olly, and children Jacqueline and Michael. So it was no surprise that when I returned to Ashington in 1982 Margaret soon came calling to welcome me back.

By that time she was a teacher at Coulson Park, a first school not far from my council flat. She knew that I was at a loose end and missing Bob and suggested that I should go along to her school as a volunteer helper to fill in some of my spare time. I imagined that I would be helping the girls with their needlework or something like that. But the boys in the class had different ideas. One day, as the children worked on their books and reading cards, I looked towards the classroom's wide windows. Outside I could see the first signs of spring approaching. Slate grey clouds, which had filled the northern sky above the school, were beginning to break up and it had stopped raining.

I wasn't the only one who had noticed. Some of the boys found the view of the school field outside far more inviting than their classwork. Eventually one of them rose from his table and approached me with a quizzical expression on his little face.

'Mrs Charlton, are you Bobby and Jack's mam?' he asked.

When I answered, 'Yes,' he smiled, clearly reassured about something and continued: 'Me Dad sez he saw your Bobby and Jack winnin' the World Cup an' he wants to know if you're teachin' us football.'

Separated by years, but united by the love of football – that's little Kerri Jobson and me.

I was taken aback at first, but then I thought, 'Why not?' I have my health and I am an active woman. If they will listen to the advice of a white-haired grandmother then I don't mind giving it.

The boys in Margaret Evans' class threw themselves into their football lessons with complete enthusiasm, especially when their dads explained to those who didn't know, the story of 1966, the World Cup and the Charltons. Only one member of the class was unhappy.

'It's not fair!' shouted little Kerri Jobson. 'Why should it be just the boys who take football?'

I was in no position to argue with her and my little team gained one more member.

Tiny Kerri, seven years old and bursting with enthusiasm for football, played as aggressively and as skilfully as the best of the boys.

She was besotted with the game and didn't mind the bumps and bruises one little bit. She gave no quarter and expected no quarter.

She was no cute little china doll lass and she had no time for namby-pamby girls' games or girls' toys.

You know, somehow, little Kerri reminds me of someone I used to know – a long, long time ago.